You're Welcome!

English for hotel reception

Shiona Harkess and Michael Wherly

Nelson

Published in association with the British Council and the Centre for British Teachers

Acknowledgements

The publishers would like to thank the following for permission to use copyright material:

Ambassador Hotel Amman; American Express; The Bloomsbury Hotel; British Airways; Hotel Borobudur Inter-Continental; Malcolm Bowen and Caterer and Hotelkeeper; Carte Blanche International Ltd; Civil Aviation Department, Hong Kong; Rank Hotels; Richard Curtis Associates Inc; Intercontinental Hotels Corporation; Hotel Jordan Inter-Continental and Lufthansa.

They would also like to express their gratitude to the staff of the Royal Lancaster Hotel, London, for all their help, in particular to Jane Baxter and Neale Monks, and to the staff of the Holiday Inn, Swiss Cottage, London.

The cover photograph was taken by Diana Lanham at the Holiday Inn, Swiss Cottage, London.

You're Welcome! and With Pleasure! are based on original material written by staff of the Centre for British Teachers for the Jordan Hotel Training Centre. The project in Jordan was funded by the British Government's Overseas Development Administration and administered by the British Council. The Jordan Ministry of Education has kindly given permission for the material to be adapted and published.

Thomas Nelson and Sons Ltd
Nelson House   Mayfield Road
Walton-on-Thames   Surrey
KT12 5PL   UK

51 York Place
Edinburgh
EH1 3JD   UK

Thomas Nelson (Hong Kong) Ltd
Toppan Building 10/F
22A Westlands Road
Quarry Bay   Hong Kong

© The British Council and the Centre for British Teachers 1984

First published by Edward Arnold

ISBN 0-7131-8131-1

This edition first published by Thomas Nelson and Sons Ltd 1991

ISBN 0-17-556246-6
NPN 9 8 7 6 5

Printed in Hong Kong

Contents

Student's Exercises   1

Reference Section

    Hotel Terms   47

    American Terms   53

    National Profiles   55

    Metric Conversion   59

    Alphabet Lists   60

_1

Listening

Did the receptionist give the guest the right time?

Role Play 1 (Stage A)

Receptionist:	Good	morning, afternoon, evening,	sir. madam.		
Guest:	Good	morning. afternoon. evening.	My name is	Brown. Thomson. Carter.	I have a reservation.

Receptionist: Excuse me one minute, | sir, madam, | while I check our list.

Oral Work

1.  2.  3.  4. 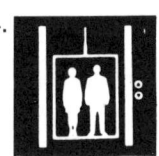 5.

Reading

The Centre for British Teachers Limited
(Limited by Guarantee)

ESP Division
Essex House
22 Crouch Street
Colchester
Essex CO3 3ES

Reservations,
Post House Hotel,
West Drayton,
Middlesex.

Tel: Colchester (0206) 67441
Telex: 987578-CESC
(Attn. ESP)

26 May, 1982

Dear Sirs,

Following my phone call today, I wish to confirm that I require a single room on the night of Tuesday, 1 June. I shall notify you if, for some reason, I cannot arrive before 6 p.m.

Please send the account to the above address.

Yours faithfully,

Michael Wherly

Michael C. Wherly

Registered English Charity No: 270901

Registered Office: Quality House, Quality Court,
Chancery Lane, London WC2A 1HP. 01-242 2982/5

Registered in England No: 867944

Listening

Write down the times with A.M. or P.M.

1. _____
2. _____
3. _____
4. _____
5. _____

6. _____
7. _____
8. _____
9. _____
10. _____

Role Play 1 (Stage B)

Receptionist: Yes, we have a reservation for you | Mr | _____.
| Mrs |
| Miss |

Would you mind filling out this form for us?

Guest: Not at all. Could you lend me a pen, please?

Receptionist: Certainly, | sir. | Here you are.
| madam. |

Guest: Thanks.

_3

Listening

Some of these guests give their names. In what order do they give them?

Bright _____	Gregg _____	Morton _____	Simpson _____
Cheyney _____	Harrison _____	Nelson _____	Sims _____
Drake _____	James _____	Norton _____	Warner _____
Gardiner _____	Morrison _____	Price _____	Wilson _____

Role Play 1 (Stage C)

Guest: Here's the form.

Receptionist: Thank you, | Mr | _____ . I'll call the | porter | to take you to
                          | Mrs |
                          | Miss | | bell-boy |

                     your room.

Guest: Good.

Receptionist: I hope you enjoy your stay here.

Reading

PLEASE PRINT USING BLOCK CAPITALS

GUESTS ARE REQUESTED TO SETTLE THEIR ACCOUNT AT THE TIME OF DEPARTURE, OR ON PRESENTATION, UNLESS PRIOR ARRANGE-MENTS HAVE BEEN AGREED. PLEASE INDICATE BELOW THE PROPOSED METHOD OF SETTLEMENT.

Cash	Cheque	Credit Card	Prior Arrangement
		✓	

TRAVELLERS CHEQUES WILL BE ACCEPTED, OTHER CHEQUES ONLY TAKEN ON PRESENTATION OF A VALID BANKERS CHEQUE CARD. GUESTS WITHOUT A CON-FIRMED RESERVATION ARE REQUIRED TO LEAVE A DEPOSIT ON ARRIVAL.

SURNAME HARKESS   MISS
                                         MR / MRS / MISS

FORENAMES SHIONA ANN MACLEOD

ADDRESS 113 ST. ADAMS ST., COLCHESTER   City / Town
           Number and Street

           ESSEX   U.K.
           County / Prov / State   Country

NATIONALITY BRITISH

CREDIT CARD VISA   No 4929-123-456-789

PASSPORT No. J 20YOG   ISSUED AT PETERBOROUGH

COMPANY: Name and Address CBT

QUALITY HOUSE., CHANCERY LANE, LONDON

FORWARDING ADDRESS AS ABOVE

SIGNATURE Shiona Ann Harkess

DATE OF DEPARTURE 10 NOV. 1983

FOLIO No.

Confirmed Reservation	Phone Reservation	Claimed Reservation	No Reservation

Safe deposits are available in the cashier's department for safe custody of valuables. All persons over the age of 16 years must be registered.

Rank Hotels

4

Oral Work

Mr Jameson is from Australia. He's Australian and his language is English. He lives in Canberra, the Capital of Australia. He often uses the National Airline: Quantas. He pays for his ticket in Australian dollars. If he wants to dial Australia from abroad he must use the prefix 61.

United States of America	France
American	French
English	French
Washington D.C.	Paris
Trans World Airlines/Pan American Airlines	Air France
Dollars	Francs
1	33

Listening

Write down the names of these guests | and their initials.

1. _____ | _____

2. _____ | _____

3. _____ | _____

4. _____ | _____

5. _____ | _____

Role Play 2 (Stage A)

Receptionist: (Greet the guest according to the time)
Can I help you?

Guest: Can I have a | single | room, please?
              | double |

Receptionist: Have you got a reservation, | sir? |
                                            | madam? |

Guest: I'm afraid I haven't.

Receptionist: I'm very sorry, | sir, | The hotel is fully booked.
                                | madam, |

Reading

  + number = number of bedrooms		Early morning tea/coffee available		Lounge available for use of guests
Licensed with bar		Light refreshments and/or bar snacks available		Children accepted all ages
Central heating in bedrooms		Packed lunches available		+number = minimum age for children
TV TV in some bedrooms on request		Choice of hot main course at evening meal		Baby listening service
R Radio in all/some bedrooms		Garden available for guests		+number = approx. distance in metres to nearest beach/lake

Sherwood Private Hotel **Harbour Avenue**	19 **TV** R 3 410
Golden Sands Hotel **113 Park Road**	10 R 95

5

Listening

Which number did they say?

13	30	31
4	14	40
15	50	53
16	60	61
7	17	70
18	80	88
9	19	91
113	130	150
104	114	140
115	116	150

Role Play 2 (Stage B)

Guest: Oh, dear. Could you recommend another hotel that won't be full up?

Receptionist: You could try the | Ambassador. | Would you like me to phone
Grand Palace.
Majestic |

them for you?

Guest: That's very kind of you.

Receptionist: Would you mind writing your name down, | sir.
madam. |

Oral Work

1983

January	February	March	April
S M T W T F S	S M T W T F S	S M T W T F S	S M T W T F S
1	1 2 3 4 5	1 2 3 4 5	1 2
2 3 4 5 6 7 8	6 7 8 9 10 11 12	6 7 8 9 10 11 12	3 4 5 6 7 8 9
9 10 11 12 13 14 15	13 14 15 16 17 18 19	13 14 15 16 17 18 19	10 11 12 13 14 15 16
16 17 18 19 20 21 22	20 21 22 23 24 25 26	20 21 22 23 24 25 26	17 18 19 20 21 22 23
23 24 25 26 27 28 29	27 28	27 28 29 30 31	24 25 26 27 28 29 30
30 31			

May	June	July	August
S M T W T F S	S M T W T F S	S M T W T F S	S M T W T F S
1 2 3 4 5 6 7	1 2 3 4	1 2	1 2 3 4 5 6
8 9 10 11 12 13 14	5 6 7 8 9 10 11	3 4 5 6 7 8 9	7 8 9 10 11 12 13
15 16 17 18 19 20 21	12 13 14 15 16 17 18	10 11 12 13 14 15 16	14 15 16 17 18 19 20
22 23 24 25 26 27 28	19 20 21 22 23 24 25	17 18 19 20 21 22 23	21 22 23 24 25 26 27
29 30 31	26 27 28 29 30	24 25 26 27 28 29 30	28 29 30 31
		31	

September	October	November	December
S M T W T F S	S M T W T F S	S M T W T F S	S M T W T F S
1 2 3	1	1 2 3 4 5	1 2 3
4 5 6 7 8 9 10	2 3 4 5 6 7 8	6 7 8 9 10 11 12	4 5 6 7 8 9 10
11 12 13 14 15 16 17	9 10 11 12 13 14 15	13 14 15 16 17 18 19	11 12 13 14 15 16 17
18 19 20 21 22 23 24	16 17 18 19 20 21 22	20 21 22 23 24 25 26	18 19 20 21 22 23 24
25 26 27 28 29 30	23 24 25 26 27 28 29	27 28 29 30	25 26 27 28 29 30 31
	30 31		

Reading

~9 JUL 1982

THE BLOOMSBURY HOTEL
9/11 Bloomsbury Square London WC1A 2NA
Telephone 01-242 5401

Mrs. H. Skeates,
The Centre for British Teachers Ltd.,
Essex House,
22, Crouch Street,
Colchester,
Essex.

Our ref: KPA/RF

3rd July 1982

Dear Mrs. Skeates,

I thank you for your letter of the 1st July 1982, and have pleasure in reserving a single bedded room for the night of Wednesday 7th July, in the name of Miss. S. Harkess.

The daily bed and breakfast tariff is £17.45 inclusive of VAT and colour T.V.

I also note that you would like the account sent to your company for payment.

I thank you for the reservation and assure you of our best attention.

Yours sincerely,

Mr. K.P. Allsopp
Hotel Manager.

Blakeney Hotels Limited   Keith Allsopp *general manager*   VAT No 233034606

Role Play 2 (Stage C)

Receptionist: Hello, is that the ＿＿＿＿ hotel? Have you got a room available?

Good. Would you reserve it in the name of ＿＿＿＿ ＿＿＿＿.

| He'll | be along in about | ten minutes. |
| She'll | | quarter of an hour. |

Guest: Thank you for your help.

Receptionist: Don't mention it, ＿＿＿＿ .

Guest: Can I get a taxi from here?

Receptionist: Yes, ＿＿＿＿ , just | outside the door. |
| in front of the hotel. |

Listening

At what time do the guests want to be called? Make a note of their room numbers.

6.00   6.15   6.30   6.45   7.00   7.15   7.30   7.45   8.00

7

Listening

Which way does the guest spell his/her name?

	A	B	C
1.	White	Whyte	
2.	Ann	Anne	
3.	Conors	Connors	
4.	Stephens	Stevens	
5.	Lawrence	Laurence	
6.	Johnson	Johnston	Johnstone
7.	Reed	Reid	Rede
8.	Davis	Davies	Daveys
9.	Meak	Meke	Meek
10.	Moriss	Morris	Morriss

Reading

Most big hotels nowadays have a telex machine. Communications by telex are instantaneous. In other words the message is received only a few seconds after it is transmitted, even if the message is being sent to the other side of the world.

The telex has many advantages over other forms of communication. It is much quicker than a letter and saves hotels a lot of time in paper work and waiting for answers to letters. It is better than the telephone because it provides a written record of the message.

A great number of advance reservations are made by telex. When advance bookings come in, the hotel replies by telex and this is the proof of booking of accommodation at the hotel.

Oral Work

Map of the World with Time Zones

Listening

Write down the names of the guests.

1. _____
2. _____
3. _____
4. _____
5. _____
6. _____
7. _____
8. _____
9. _____
10. _____

Reading

```
8954262RLANC G
874451 HLTD UR

OUR REF 2456/JD

ATTENTION OF ADVANCE RESERVATIONS

YOU ARE HOLDING ONE DOUBLE ROOM ON THE 7TH DECEMBER FOR
MR AND MRS N DICKENS BUT DUE TO TRAVEL COMMITMENTS THEY CANNOT NOW
VISIT LONDON AS PLANNED.

COULD YOU KINDLY THEREFORE CANCEL THEIR RESERVATION.

SORRY FOR ANY INCONVENIENCE THAT THIS MAY HAVE CAUSED.

MANY THANKS.
JODIE ALLEN      HOTELS UNLIMITED

8954262 RLANC G
874451 HLTD UR


8954262RLANC G
865432 WAKEF UR

8/10/82    MESSAGE TIMED  15.50 HRS    REF. 2456

MESSAGE FOR ROYAL LANCASTER HOTEL    LONDON

FROM WAKEFIELD FROST INFORMATION SERVICES OF DETROIT

URGENTLY REQUEST YOU TO AMEND THE RESERVATION YOU ARE HOLDING FOR
MESSRS J PERKINS AND N GOLDMAN IN ONE TWIN ROOM TO NOW COMMENCE 2
NIGHTS EARLIER.

RESERVATION WAS ORIGINALLY FOR OCT. 11 UNTIL OCT 21.  PLEASE REPLY
TO TELEX NUMBER 865432 AS SOON AS POSSIBLE.

THANK YOU AND REGARDS
K WISEMAN

8954262RLANC G
865432 WAKEF UR
```

Listening

Which keys do the guests want?

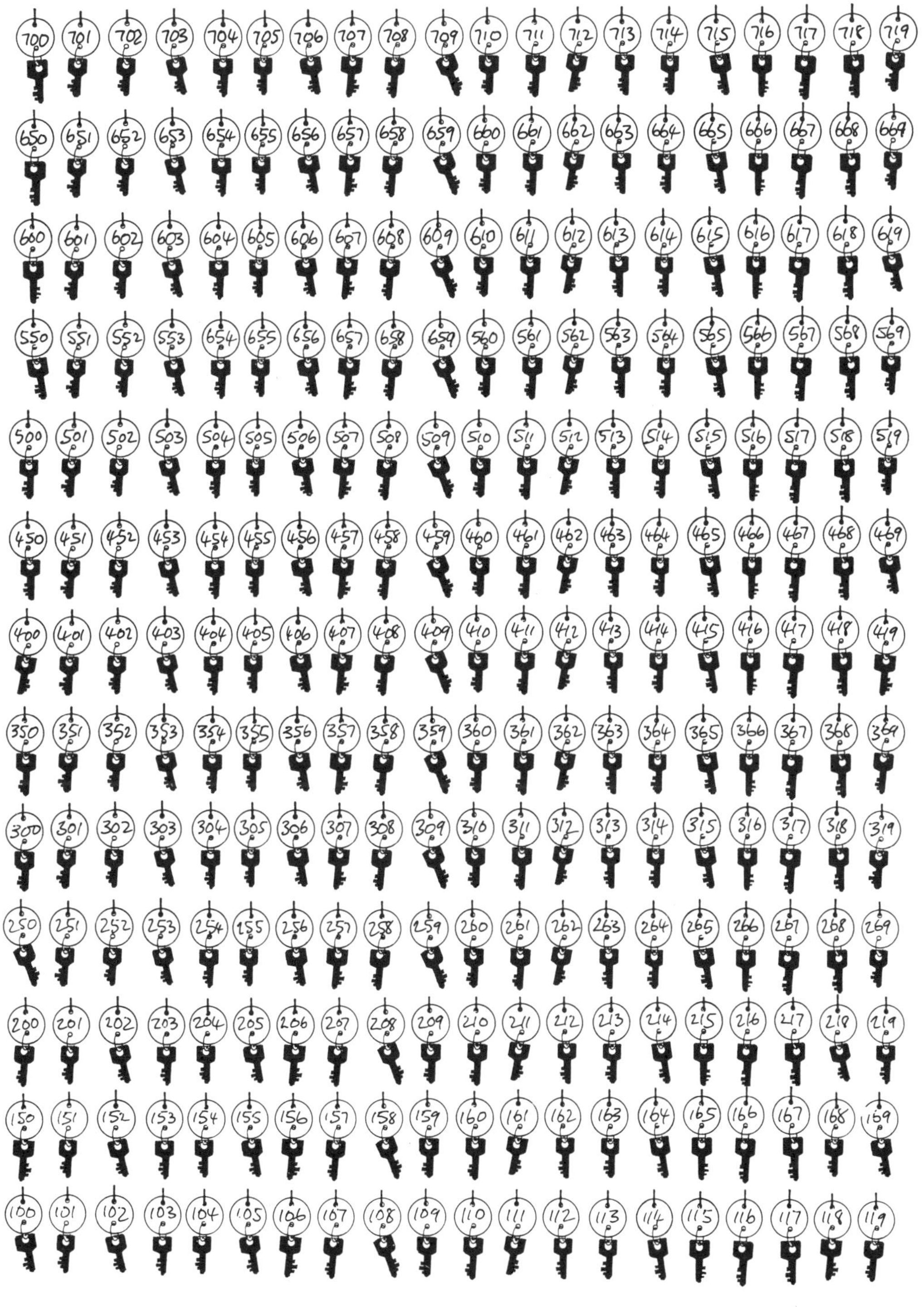

700	701	702	703	704	705	706	707	708	709	710	711	712	713	714	715	716	717	718	719
650	651	652	653	654	655	656	657	658	659	600	661	662	663	664	665	666	667	668	669
660	601	602	603	604	605	606	607	608	609	610	611	612	613	614	615	616	617	618	619
550	551	552	553	654	655	656	657	658	659	560	561	562	563	564	565	566	567	568	569
500	501	502	503	504	505	506	507	508	509	510	511	512	513	514	515	516	517	518	519
450	451	452	453	454	455	456	457	458	459	460	461	462	463	464	465	466	467	468	469
400	401	402	403	404	405	406	407	408	409	410	411	412	413	414	415	416	417	418	419
350	351	352	353	354	355	356	357	358	359	360	361	362	363	364	365	366	367	368	369
300	301	302	303	304	305	306	307	308	309	310	311	312	313	314	315	316	317	318	319
250	251	252	253	254	155	256	257	258	259	260	261	262	263	264	265	266	267	268	269
200	201	202	203	204	205	206	207	208	209	210	211	212	213	214	215	216	217	218	219
150	151	152	153	154	155	156	157	158	159	160	161	162	163	164	165	166	167	168	169
100	101	102	103	104	105	106	107	108	109	110	111	112	113	114	115	116	117	118	119

Role Play 3 (Stage A)

Guest: | Hey, you there. |
| Excuse me. |
| *(knock on desk)* |

Receptionist: I'm | very | sorry, _____ . I didn't
| terribly |

| realise there was anyone there. |
| hear you come to the desk. |

Guest: That's all right. Can I have a _____ room?

| | haven't booked. |
| | don't have a reservation. |

Receptionist: I'll see | if we have a vacancy, | _____ .
| what we have, |

Listening

Write down these room numbers.

1. _____
2. _____
3. _____
4. _____
5. _____

6. _____
7. _____
8. _____
9. _____
10. _____

Reading

**PLEASE SHOW THIS CARD
EACH TIME YOU
COLLECT YOUR KEY**

Name ....

Room No. ....

Rate ....
including service charge and VAT at 15%.
This rate does not include breakfast.

Date Out ....
Guests are requested to vacate their rooms
by 12 noon on the day of their departure.

WE STRONGLY RECOMMEND THAT YOU:

Secure your bedroom door lock
Press in the centre button on the handle. This prevents
entry from the outside. To cancel lock turn door handle.

Advise our medical department
Or the Duty Manager if you require medical attention
or are already under medical care by dialling 0.

Emergency
Dial 555, state your room number and the assistance
that you require.

RESTAURANTS & BARS

"La Rosette" Restaurant
on the 1st floor overlooking the Italian
Gardens of Hyde Park. A superb
international restaurant offering full à la
carte or typical English dishes.

The Mediterranean Café
on the 1st floor, luxurious surroundings
to enjoy a sophisticated cocktail.

Banqueting
Private dining and conference rooms are
available for your parties or meetings.

Telex and Telegrams
For prompt national and international
communications, Telex 8954262
(RLANC). Forms at Reception.

Shops
Shops are situated in the Front Lobby.

Car Parking
Car parking facilities are available on the
2nd floor.

11

Listening

When are these services available? Write the A.M./P.M. times.

A. Breakfast   is served from _____ to _____

B. Lunch   is served from _____ to _____

C. Dinner   is served from _____ to _____

D. The Bar   is open from _____ to _____

E. The Shop   is open from _____ to _____

F. The Beauty Salon   is open from _____ to _____

G. The Disco   is open from _____ to _____

H. The Travel Agent   is open from _____ to _____

Role Play 3 (Stage B)

Receptionist: Yes, _____ . | We do have a vacancy. | There is a room available. |

Guest: | How much is it? | What does it cost? | What are your rates? |

Receptionist: | 12 | dinars | a night. | 15 | francs | 25 | pounds |

Guest: Does that include breakfast?

Receptionist: I'm afraid not, _____ .

Guest: All right, I'll take it.

Receptionist: Can I have your name, _____ ?

Guest: _____ .

Receptionist: | Would you mind spelling | that for me? | Could you please spell |

Guest: Certainly. _____ .

Oral Work

1.    2.    3.    4.    5.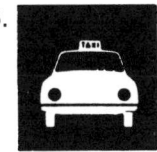

12

Listening

Which rooms are these guest talking about?

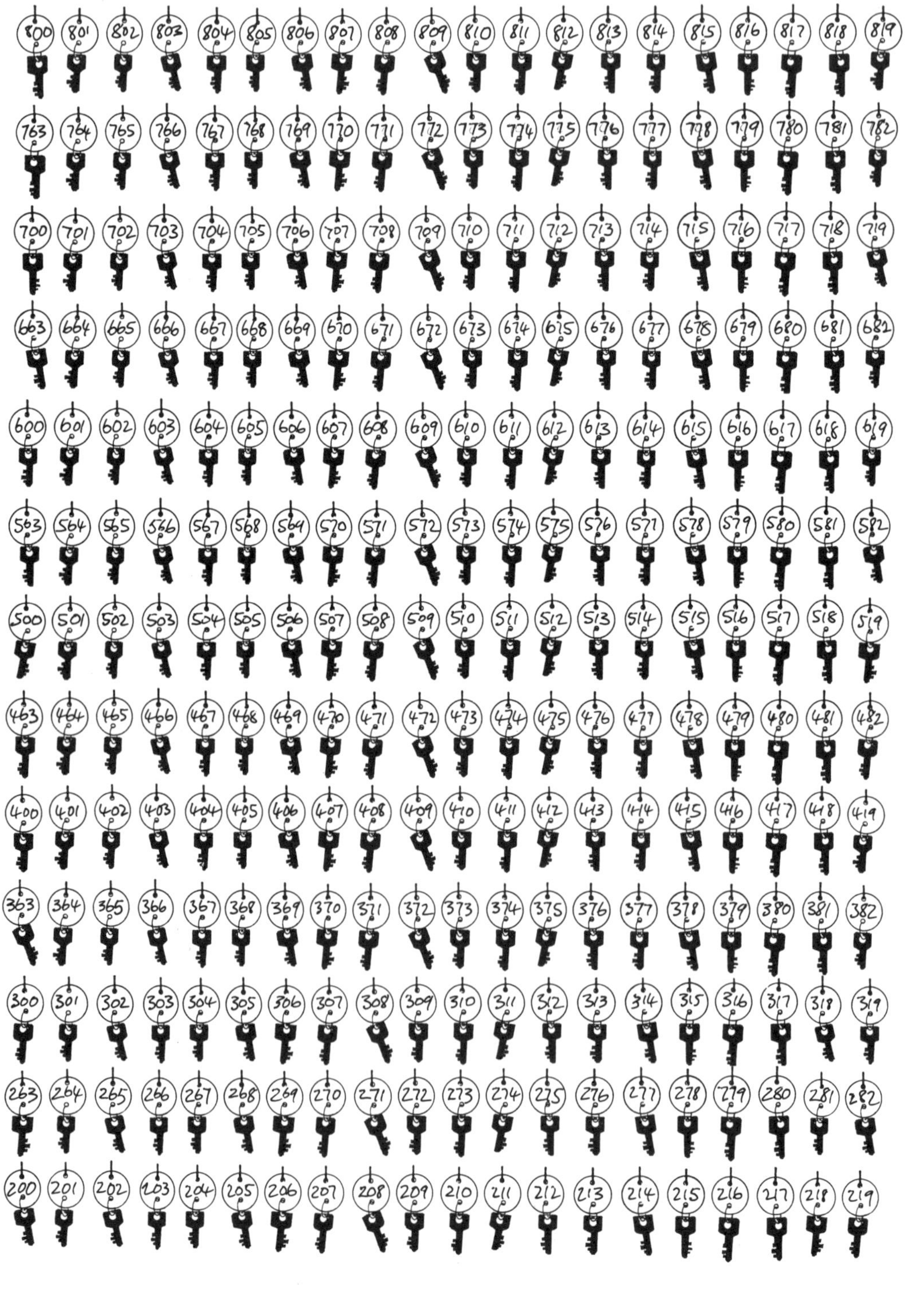

800 801 802 803 804 805 806 807 808 809 810 811 812 813 814 815 816 817 818 819

763 764 765 766 767 768 769 770 771 772 773 774 775 776 777 778 779 780 781 782

700 701 702 703 704 705 706 707 708 709 710 711 712 713 714 715 716 717 718 719

663 664 665 666 667 668 669 670 671 672 673 674 675 676 677 678 679 680 681 682

600 601 602 603 604 605 606 607 608 609 610 611 612 613 614 615 616 617 618 619

563 564 565 566 567 568 569 570 571 572 573 574 575 576 577 578 579 580 581 582

500 501 502 503 504 505 506 507 508 509 510 511 512 513 514 515 516 517 518 519

463 464 465 466 467 468 469 470 471 472 473 474 475 476 477 478 479 480 481 482

400 401 402 403 404 405 406 407 408 409 410 411 412 413 414 415 416 417 418 419

363 364 365 366 367 368 369 370 371 372 373 374 375 376 377 378 379 380 381 382

300 301 302 303 304 305 306 307 308 309 310 311 312 313 314 315 316 317 318 319

263 264 265 266 267 268 269 270 271 272 273 274 275 276 277 278 279 280 281 282

200 201 202 203 204 205 206 207 208 209 210 211 212 213 214 215 216 217 218 219

13

Role Play 3 (Stage C)

Receptionist: How long | do you expect | to stay, _____ ?
| would you like |

Guest: Until the _____ .

Receptionist: | Would | you fill in the registration form, please.
| Could |

Guest: | Certainly. |
| Right. |

Receptionist: I'm afraid | we have to ask for | a deposit of _____ .
| there will be |

Guest: | That's all right. | I'll have to | cash a travellers cheque.
| Oh, I see. | | change some money.

Reading

Most hotels have a list of all people who are not welcome. There are many reasons why someone may not be welcome. Maybe the person has not paid his bill after a stay at the hotel in the past. Perhaps he got drunk or destroyed hotel furnishings. He might have made a lot of noise or bothered other guests.

In most hotels the Black List is taped inside a cupboard so that you can look at it without the person knowing what you are doing. You should never say: 'We don't want you here!' It is better to say: 'We don't have any vacancies, I'm afraid.' In the case of this person, this is true.

It is important that the Black List is kept safely. The names are confidential and it is better if very few people know about it.

Listening

What are the missing words?

1. Your room's on the (a) _____ floor, isn't it?

   No, it's on the (b) _____ floor.

2. Is the restaurant on the ground floor or the (a) _____ floor?

   You're the (b) _____ guest that has asked me that today.

   It's on the (c) _____ floor.

3. This is my (a) _____ day here and I still don't have a drinking-glass.

   I'm sorry but this is only my (b) _____ day here. I'll get you one immediately.

4. This is my (a) _____ birthday.

   I hope you will be around for your (b) _____ .

Listening

What are the room numbers of these guests?

A.   J. Azikwe
B.   J. Bamburger
C.   Judith Cork
D.   John Dawson

E.   V. Dubois
F.   Pedro Gonzalas
G.   Steven Hasoloan
H.   Frank Smith
I.   P. Van der Palme

Role Play 4 (Stage A)

Guest: *(Greet the receptionist according to the time.)*

| You have a booking for me. |
| I have a reservation. |

Receptionist: *(Return the guest's greeting.)* | What is / May I have | your name, _____ .

Guest: I'm | Mr / Mrs / Miss | _____ .

Receptionist: Would you | excuse me for one / mind waiting a | minute, / moment, | _____ | I'll just / while I |

check our list.

Reading

Many guests prefer to carry their money in the form of travellers cheques because these are safer than cash. If the guest loses them, or if they are stolen, he can get his money back. Travellers cheques have other advantages. They can be bought in different kinds of currency, so the guest does not have to worry about changing rates of exchange. Also, if the travellers cheques are issued by a reputable company, the guest will have no difficulty in exchanging them for cash at hotels and shops. He does not have to go to a bank to change them.

When a person buys travellers cheques, he must sign them in front of the bank cashier. If a guest wishes to change a travellers cheque at your hotel, you must watch him countersign the cheque. You must then compare the two signatures and make sure they are both the same. You should also ask the guest to give you proof of his identity by showing you his passport, or some other official document with his name and signature on it.

Role Play 4 (Stage B)

Receptionist: | Could you give me | your initial _____ _____ ?
| What is

Guest: _____ .

Receptionist: Ah, yes. You're in room | 614. | Would you mind filling up |
| 517. | Could you please fill out |
| etc. |

this form for us.

Guest: | All right. | Do you | need | my passport?
| O.K. | | want |

Receptionist: No, | that's not necessary, | _____ .
| we don't need it,

Listening

Write down these telephone numbers.

1. _____   7. _____
2. _____   8. _____
3. _____   9. _____
4. _____   10. _____
5. _____   11. _____
6. _____   12. _____

Reading

Lakes and Mountains

Grand Hotel Villa Serbelloni, Bellagio

This palatial lakeside hotel is situated on the tip of the Bellagio peninsula. The elegant, lofty public rooms have chandeliers hanging from painted ceilings and are exquisitely furnished. They include lounges, a bar, a restaurant and a breakfast room. There is a lift service to the bedrooms. There is evening dancing to an orchestra and a feature of the hotel is the large swimming pool in a garden setting, alongside the private beach and lakeside. This is a highly recommended hotel in the old style.

Twin bedded rooms with private bath or shower and wc. Twin bedded rooms with bath, wc and lake view, supplement £52 per person per week. Single rooms with bath or shower and wc, supplement £35 per week.
Half board. *Supplement for full board £32 per person per week.*

Hotel Bella Vista, Menaggio

A small, traditional style hotel right on the lakeside at Menaggio, the Bella Vista is modest, with a very friendly atmosphere, and the owner-manager prides himself on giving personal service. There is a delightful restaurant with an open air terrace which looks out across the lake. Rear rooms at the hotel overlook the main road. The ferry landing stage is only five minutes walk away, making the hotel a convenient base for sightseeing.

Twin bedded rooms with private bath or shower and wc. Twin bedded rooms with bath or shower, wc and lake view, supplement £17 per person per week. Single rooms with shower and wc, supplement £17 per week.
Half board. *Supplement for full board £16 per person per week.*

Listening

Write down the passport details of these guests.

1. Passport Number _____
   Date of Issue _____
   Place of Issue _____
2. Passport Number _____
   Date of Issue _____
   Place of Issue _____

3. Passport Number _____
   Date of Issue _____
   Place of Issue _____
4. Passport Number _____
   Date of Issue _____
   Place of Issue _____

Role Play 4 (Stage C)

Guest: Here's the form.

Receptionist: Thank you, _____ . I'll call the | porter | to
| bell-boy |

| show you to your room. |
| take your cases up. |

Guest: What | did you say my room number was? |
| was the room number again? |

Receptionist: | 614, | _____ . That's on the | sixth | floor.
| 517, | | fifth |
| etc. | | fourth |

The | porter | will show you the way.
| bell-boy |

Guest: Thank you. Good night.

Receptionist: Good night, _____ . I hope you sleep well.

Oral Work

Inclusive Prices per person in Pounds (from London Heathrow)	**British Airways Flights to Hong Kong** Departures from London Heathrow every Thursday														
Departures	1 Nov to 17 Dec			18 to 31 Dec			1 to 31 Jan			1 Feb to 12 Mar			13 to 26 Mar		
Hol No No of Nights	7	14	21	7	14	21	7	14	21	7	14	21	7	14	21
Q6202 **Park**	570	665	760	590	685	775	580	670	765	560	650	750	590	680	770
Q6205 **Lee Gardens**	590	695	815	610	710	820	600	700	820	580	685	795	600	710	820
Q6207 **Royal Garden**	650	795	950	660	805	960	650	795	950	625	775	925	650	795	950
Q6203 **Mandarin**	720	950	1170	730	960	1180	725	950	1175	700	925	1150	725	950	1175
Q6220 **Canton Tour & Park**	—	795	890	—	805	900	—	800	895	—	795	890	—	805	900
Q6218 **or Lee Gardens**	—	830	935	—	840	945	—	825	935	—	810	915	—	830	940
Q6223 **or Royal Garden**	—	910	1055	—	915	1065	—	905	1050	—	880	1035	—	910	1045
Q6208 **or Mandarin**	—	1035	1255	—	1050	1265	—	1035	1250	—	1015	1235	—	1035	1200

Travel Details	Depart London Heathrow 1155 hrs (approx) Arrive back London Heathrow 0505 hrs (approx) Sat
	Flying time London/Hong Kong 16 hours (approx)
	Airport taxes – see page 6 for important note.
CHILD REDUCTIONS	Infants under 2 years. Air travel and cot charge £50
	2-8 years inclusive 20%; 9-11 years inclusive 15% (Children under 12 years are not accepted on Canton Tours)
Reductions for 3rd person	12 years and over (only applicable when sharing 3 bedded room) 10%

17

Listening

What kind of money are these guests talking about? Write the number beside the right currency.

A. dollars _____   G. pesetas _____

B. drachmas_____   H. pesos _____

C. francs _____   I. riyals _____

D. guilders _____   J. roubles _____

E. krona _____   K. rupees _____

F. marks _____   L. yen _____

Reading

In the past, the accounts of hotel guests were kept in a ledger, known as the visitors' tabular ledger, or 'tab'. Whenever bills or dockets were received from the various departments, the front office staff would enter the transaction into this ledger. Guests' bills were prepared from these entries in the 'tab'.

Small hotels still use this method of keeping the accounts of their guests, but in larger hotels the 'tab' has been replaced by a computer. A computer can store a great deal of information and it can give back this data much more quickly than a person can. For example, it can tell immediately how many rooms are available at that time, or how many guests will arrive on a certain date, as well as keeping up-to-the-minute accounts of guests' purchases. Information is fed into the computer by using a keyboard, like a typewriter. This keyboard is also used to find out information from the computer. The information may be displayed on a screen, or it may be printed out. In this way the computer has made the clerical work of the receptionist and the cashier much easier and quicker.

Role Play 5 (Stage A)

Cashier: Can I help you, _____ ?

Guest: Yes, I'd like to | pay | my | bill. | I'm | leaving |
                           | settle | | account. | | checking out |

                     | in an hour's time. |
                     | at half past four. |

Cashier: I'll get it ready for you | straight away, | _____ .
                                         | immediately, |

         You're in room _____ , aren't you?

Guest: That's right.

Cashier: Have you | used your mini-bar | since breakfast, _____ ?
                     | ordered from room service |
                     | signed for anything |

Guest: No, I haven't.

Cashier: Here's your | account, | _____ .
                   | bill, |

Guest: | Let me just | check it first.
        | I'd better |

Role Play 5 (Stage B)

Guest: Excuse me, what's this | item | here?
| charge |
| sum |

Cashier: That's for the | restaurant.
| room service.
| (mini) bar.

Guest: But that's for the | 22nd. | That was | Monday, | wasn't it?
| 8th. | | Thursday, |

I | was away all day | that day.
| wasn't here |

Cashier: I'll go and check that immediately _____ . | I'm very sorry,
| We do apologise,

you're quite right. | We made a mistake.
| It was an error.

Listening

Which floor are these rooms on?

A. Petra Suite

B. Beauty Parlour

C. Conference Rooms

D. Banqueting Hall

E. Games Room

F. Sauna

G. Disco

H. Cocktail Lounge

Oral Work

1.  2.  3.  4.  5.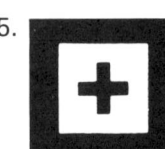

Listening

How much money do these guests want to change?

A. _____	$US	G. _____	Fr. Fr.
B. _____	$Can.	H. _____	Sw. Fr.
C. _____	$S	I. _____	L. lt.
D. _____	$Aus.	J. _____	Pts.
E. _____	£	K. _____	D.Kr.
F. _____	DM	L. _____	Gld.

Oral Work

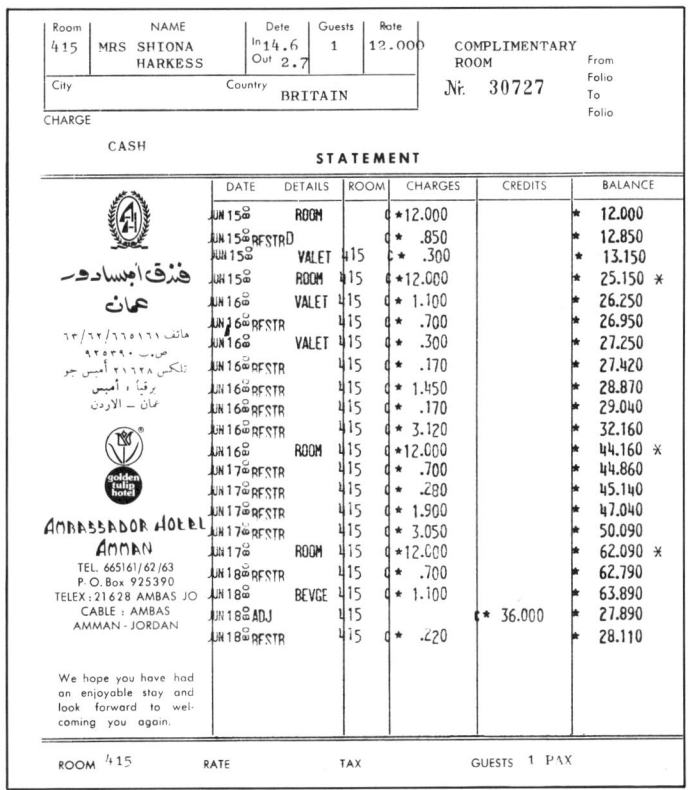

Role Play 5 (Stage C)

Guest:
That seems right now.	How much is _____	francs	in
Yes, that's correct.		riyals	
		guilders	

| US dollars? |
| pounds? |
| marks? |

Cashier: At _____ to the _____ that'll be . . . let me see . . . _____ _____ .

Guest: Right. I'll change some travellers cheques.

20

Listening

Which embassy do these guests want to go to?

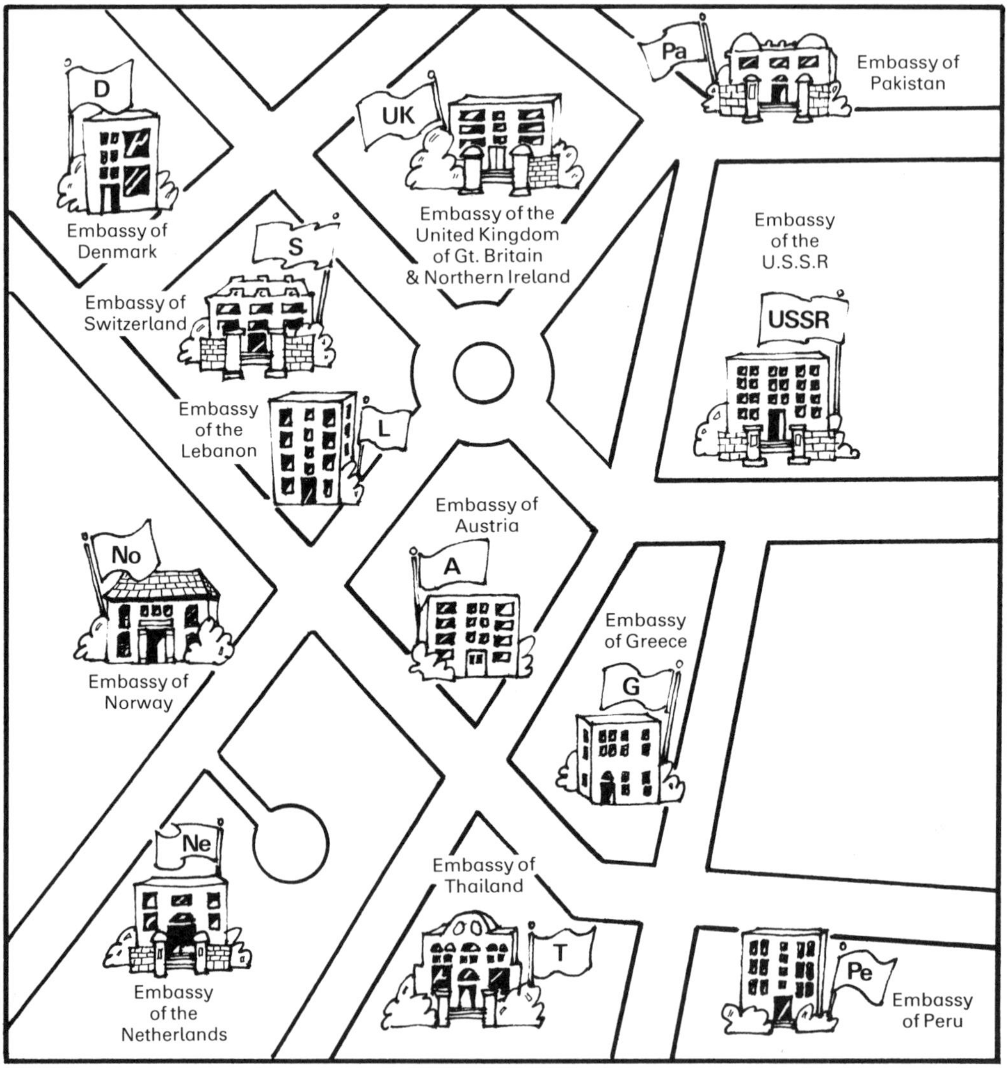
D
Embassy of Denmark
UK
Embassy of the United Kingdom of Gt. Britain & Northern Ireland
Pa
Embassy of Pakistan
S
Embassy of Switzerland
Embassy of the U.S.S.R
USSR
L
Embassy of the Lebanon
Embassy of Austria
A
No
Embassy of Norway
Embassy of Greece
G
Ne
Embassy of the Netherlands
Embassy of Thailand
T
Pe
Embassy of Peru

Role Play 6 (Stage A)

Cashier: *(Greet the guest.)* Can I help you?

Guest: | Can I / Do you | change | travellers cheques / money | here?

Cashier: | Certainly, / By all means, | ______ . What would you like?

Guest: What is the rate of exchange on the | dollar? / pound? / mark? |

Cashier: It's ______ to the ______ .

Listening

Which part of the hotel are these guests talking about?

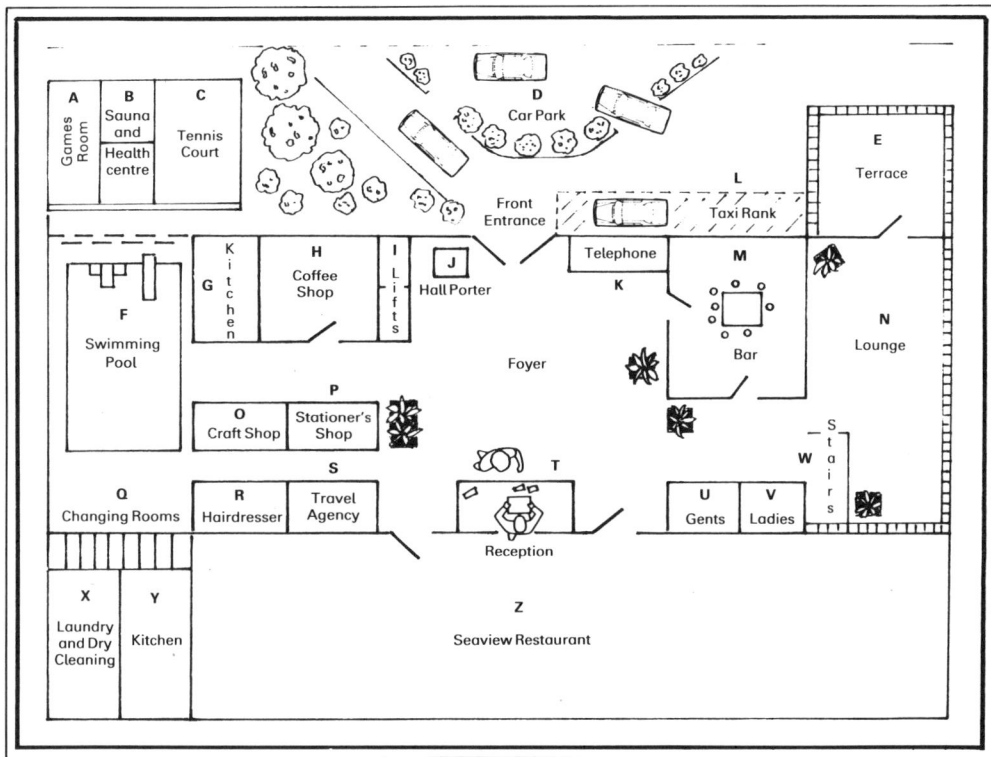

Role Play 6 (Stage B)

Guest: | You don't give | a very good rate. I got more at the bank
| That's not |

the other day.

Cashier: I'm very sorry, _____ . I'm afraid hotels have to add a charge for providing this service.

Guest: Oh, I see. Well, in that case, I'll | only | change | 20 | _____ till I can
| just | | 50 |

get to the bank.

Cashier: Very well, _____ | 20 | _____ , that will be _____
| 50 |

and _____ .

Guest: | Fine. | Do you | need | my passport?
| O.K. | | want |

Cashier: No, | it's not necessary. | Here you are, _____ .
| that's all right. |

Role Play 7 (Stage A)

Guest: Look here. I've been | waiting | here for | ages.
| standing | | 10 minutes. |

Isn't anybody going to attend to me?

Receptionist: I'll be with you | just as soon as I can, | _____ . Would you like to
| in just one minute, |

fill in this registration form | in the meantime. |
| while you're waiting. |

Guest: Now, at last, we're getting somewhere.

Receptionist: I'm sorry you've | been kept waiting, | _____ . We're | rather |
| had to wait so long, | | very |

busy | just now. |
| at the moment. |

Guest: Yes, I can see that. Here's the registration form.

Receptionist: Thank you, _____ . I'll just get your key.

Listening

How do these guests want to pay their bills? Is the method of payment acceptable?

Credit Cards	Guest Number	Acceptable	Not Acceptable
A. American Express	_____	_____	_____
B. Diners Club	_____	_____	_____
C. Access	_____	_____	_____
D. Visa	_____	_____	_____
E. Carte Blanche	_____	_____	_____
F. British Airways	_____	_____	_____
G. Bankamericard	_____	_____	_____
Cheques			
H. Personal Cheques	_____	_____	_____
I. Eurocheques	_____	_____	_____
J. Travellers Cheques	_____	_____	_____

Reading

It is very important that hotel staff should be polite and helpful to their guests. This is easy when the guests are also polite and easy to deal with. But what happens when the opposite is true? What happens when a guest is rude and abusive? It is an art to be nice to such people. This art can be learnt. Training can help you to deal with rude and abusive guests. You must listen to the guest and sympathize with his or her problem. 'If handled properly a complaint can become a compliment,' says a training manager for a big hotel group. And if you can handle difficult guests it will give you a lot of satisfaction. The best thing anybody can say about a hotel is that it is 'a home from home.' A hotel with courteous, friendly staff is just that.

Listening

Are these statements about the plan true or false?

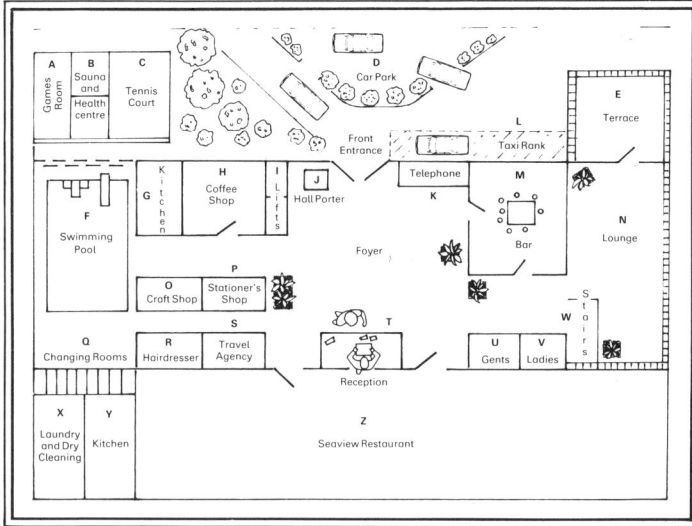

1. True/False

2. True/False

3. True/False

4. True/False

5. True/False

6. True/False

7. True/False

8. True/False

Role Play 7 (Stage B)

Receptionist: Oh, excuse me, _____ . You | haven't filled in | this section
forgot to complete |

here. How | do you wish | to pay your | bill?
would you like | | account?

Guest: I'll pay with my | Carte Blanche | card.
Diners
Visa

Receptionist: I'm very sorry, _____ , we don't accept _____ .

Guest: You don't accept credit cards?

Receptionist: I'm afraid the only credit card we accept is American Express.

Reading

(a) Check that the card is a valid, unexpired Carte Blanche Card. (All Carte Blanche cards begin with the number "9" and have ten digits.)

(b) Always check the expiration date.

(c) The signature panel on all cards is on the *reverse* side of the card.

24

Listening

What electrical fault are these guests complaining about?

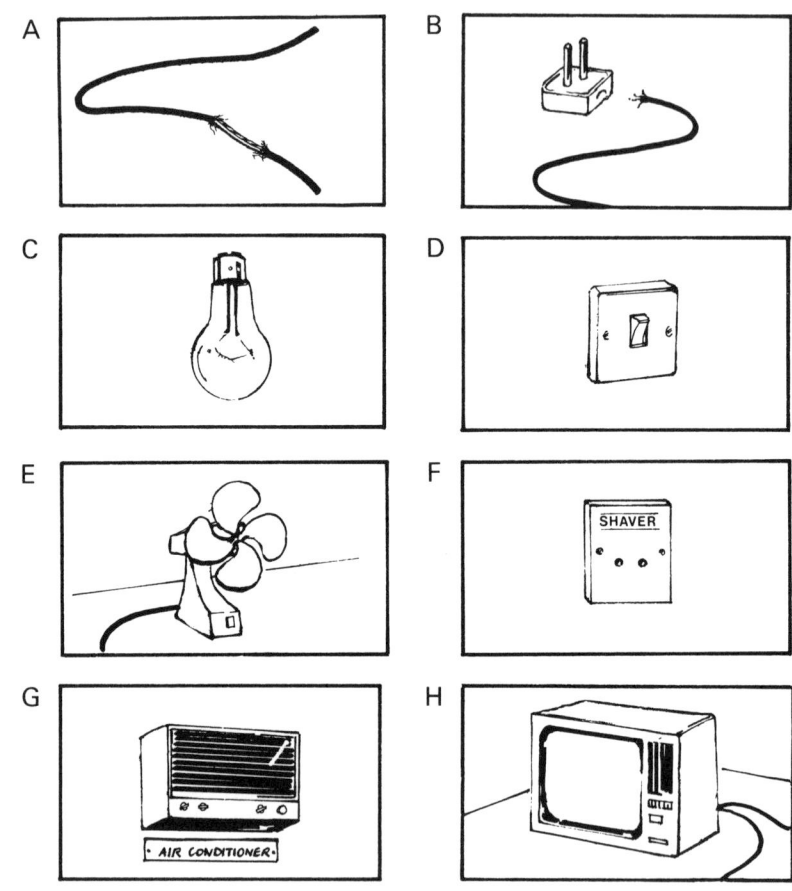

A

B

C

D

E

F

G

H

Role Play 7 (Stage C)

Guest: Well, I | don't have | an American Express card. Can I pay by
| haven't got |

personal cheque?

Receptionist: How long | are you staying, | _____ ?
| will you be here, |

Guest: Two days.

Receptionist: We | normally | need longer to clear a personal cheque.
| usually |

| Perhaps you should have a word with | our Credit Manager?
| Would you like to speak to |

25

Listening

What plumbing faults are these guests complaining about?

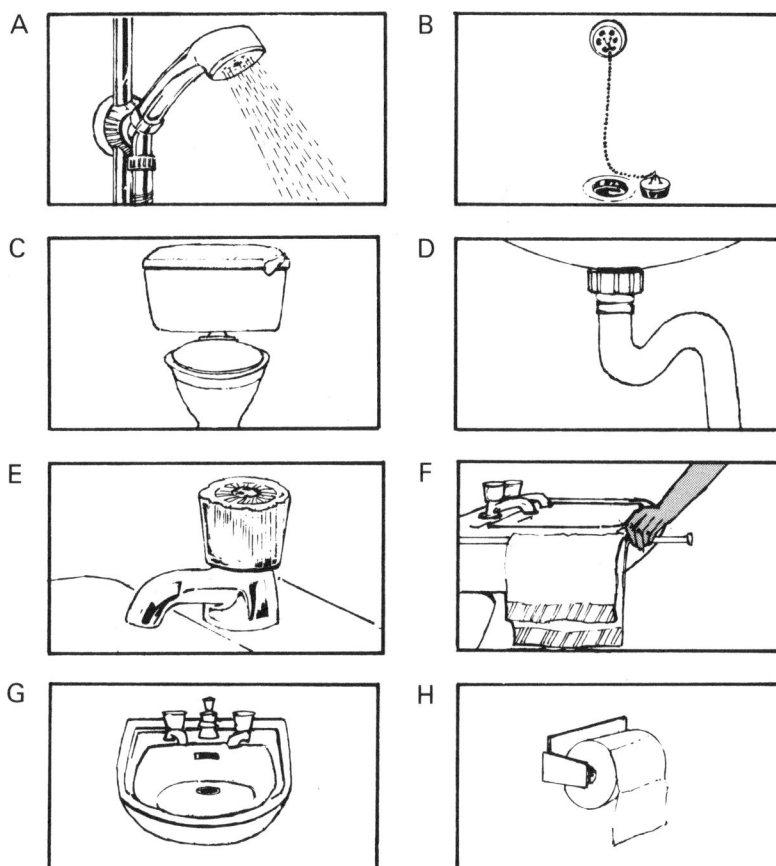

A   B

C   D

E   F

G   H

Reading

Comments from our guests help us to maintain the courteous and efficient hospitality associated with Inter•Continental Hotels around the world. We ask that you take a few moments to complete this questionnaire and give us any suggestions you may have for enhancing our service.

Please leave this questionnaire at the Reception Desk for the General Manager or, if you prefer, send it to my attention at: Thank you for having chosen this Hotel. We hope you have enjoyed your stay and look forward to serving you again at this and other Inter•Continental Hotels.

3. Guest Room

Guest Room number this visit: *634*

A. Did you find this room:

Well furnished and comfortable .... Yes ☑   No ☐

Adequately supplied with hangers, ashtrays,

stationery, etc. .... ☑   ☐

Well cleaned .... ☑   ☐

B. Did you find your bathroom:

Adequately supplied with towels, soap, etc. .... ☑   ☐

Well cleaned .... ☑   ☐

C. Is there anything you would like changed or added

in your guestroom? .... ☑   ☐

If "Yes," please specify: *Stronger bulbs in the bedside lamps.*

Role Play 8 (Stage A)

Receptionist: *(Greet the caller.)* Can I help you?

Caller: Yes, I'd like to | reserve | a room for a friend, please.
| book |

Receptionist: Certainly, _____ single or double?

Caller: _____ , with bath of course.

Receptionist: For what dates, _____ ?

Caller: From the | 1st | of | June | until the _____ of _____ .
| 10th | | July |
| 28th | | August |

(Excuse yourself while you check the list.)

Listening

What faults in their room are these guests complaining about?

A 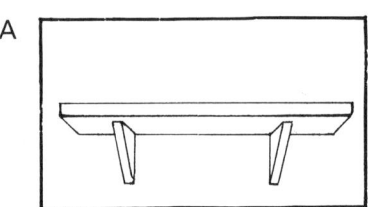 B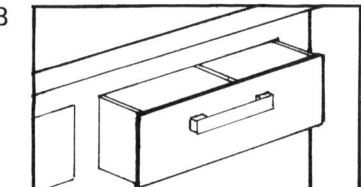

C 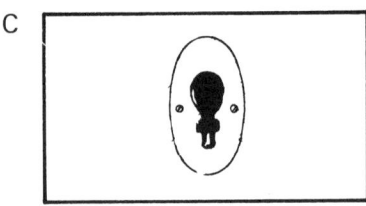 D

E 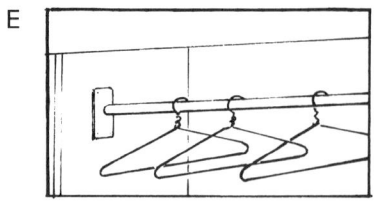 F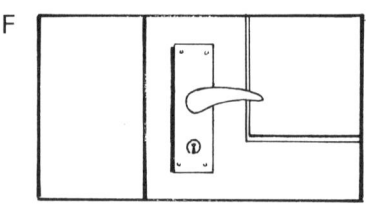

G 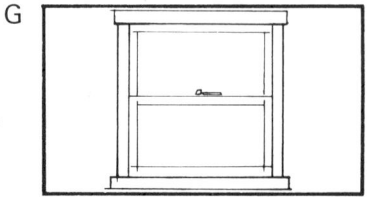 H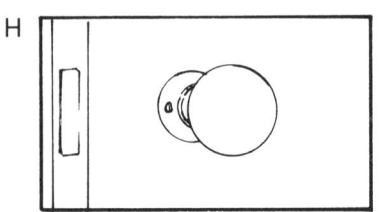

Listening

Where do the guests want to go?

A Post Office

B Ladies' Dress Shop

G Dentist's Surgery

H Jeweller's

C Shoe Shop

D Flying Carpet Night Club

E Peacock Restaurant

I Supermarket

J Furniture Shop

F Stationer's

K Doctor's Surgery

L Exchange Bureau

M Immigration Office

Role Play 8 (Stage B)

Receptionist: That will be all right, _____ . | Can I have / Could you give me | the name of the guest?

Caller: _____ .

Receptionist: | Would you mind spelling / Could you please spell | that for me?

Caller: _____ . | What are your rates, / How much do you charge, | by the way?

Receptionist: _____ a night. Will that be all right?

Caller: I expect so.

Oral Work

1
2.
3
4.
5

Listening

Where can these guests be contacted?

1.
GUEST . . . .
Room No. . . . .
is at present

☐   at the pool
☐   in the restaurant
☐   in the bar
☐   in the coffee shop
☐   in the lounge

2.
GUEST . . . .
Room No. . . . .
is at present

☐   at the pool
☐   in the restaurant
☐   in the bar
☐   in the coffee shop
☐   in the lounge

3.
GUEST . . . .
Room No. . . . .
is at present

☐   at the pool
☐   in the restaurant
☐   in the bar
☐   in the coffee shop
☐   in the lounge

4.
GUEST . . . .
Room No. . . . .
is at present

☐   at the pool
☐   in the restaurant
☐   in the bar
☐   in the coffee shop
☐   in the lounge

5.
GUEST . . . .
Room No. . . . .
is at present

☐   at the pool
☐   in the restaurant
☐   in the bar
☐   in the coffee shop
☐   in the lounge

6.
GUEST . . . .
Room No. . . . .
is at present

☐   at the pool
☐   in the restaurant
☐   in the bar
☐   in the coffee shop
☐   in the lounge

Role Play 8 (Stage C)

Caller: | Will | you write to _____ and confirm the booking?
            | Could |

Receptionist: Certainly, _____ . | What address should we write to? |
                              | Where shall we send the letter? |

Caller: To _____ .

Receptionist: *(Check the spelling, if necessary, then repeat the address.)*

                 Is that _____ ?

Caller: | Yes, that's right. |
               | No, it's _____ . |

Receptionist: Very well, _____ . We'll send a letter off tomorrow.

Listening

Make a note of these reservations.

1.							
____ sgl. ____ dbl. ____ st. conf. recep.	with	bath AC CH TV	for	____ nts. ____ wks. ____ gsts. ____ dys.	from . . . . till . . . . on . . . .
2.					
____ sgl. ____ dbl. ____ st. conf. recep.	with	bath AC CH TV	for	____ nts. ____ wks. ____ gsts. ____ dys.	from . . . . till . . . . on . . . .
3.					
____ sgl. ____ dbl. ____ st. conf. recep.	with	bath AC CH TV	for	____ nts. ____ wks. ____ gsts. ____ dys.	from . . . . till . . . . on . . . .
4.					
____ sgl. ____ dbl. ____ st. conf. recep.	with	bath AC CH TV	for	____ nts. ____ wks. ____ gsts. ____ dys.	from . . . . till . . . . on . . . .
5.					
____ sgl. ____ dbl. ____ st. conf. recep.	with	bath AC CH TV	for	____ nts. ____ wks. ____ gsts. ____ dys.	from . . . . till . . . . on . . . .

Reading

```
8954262RLANC G
245877 SSALD G


ATTN OF RECEPTION/RESERVATIONS
WE WOULD LIKE TO BOOK ONE SUITE FOR THE 28TH NOVEMBER FOR 3 NIGHTS
IN THE NAME OF CAPT. AND MRS W PROCTOR-STEWART.
THEY HAVE STAYED IN YOUR HOTEL MANY TIMES AND AS THIS IS THEIR 25TH
WEDDING ANNIVERSARY THIS IS THEIR FIRST CHOICE.
COULD YOU PLEASE ARRANGE FOR A BOUQUET OF FLOWERS AND A BOTTLE OF
CHAMPAGNE TO BE PLACED IN THEIR ROOM ON ARRIVAL TO THE VALUE OF
APPROXIMATELY 30.00 POUNDS.
PLEASE PLACE A MESSAGE WITH THE ABOVE TO READ 'CONGRATULATIONS AND
SEE YOU ON SUNDAY, KITTIE AND DAVID'.
PLEASE RE CONFIRM THAT ALL THE ABOVE CAN BE ARRANGED SO THAT WE CAN
FORWARD A DEPOSIT TO YOU AS SOON AS POSSIBLE.
LOOKING FORWARD TO YOUR CONFIRMATION.
MRS K EDWARDSON
TRAVEL MANAGER
SAINT SALDRON TRAVEL
21 LEWISH PARK AVENUE
BRADFORD
```

Listening

Write down these messages.

1.
TELEPHONE MESSAGE
FOR *Mr. Robinson* ......
ROOM ....
FROM ....
....
....
....

4.
TELEPHONE MESSAGE
FOR *Mr. Rossi* ....
ROOM ....
FROM ....
....
....
....

2.
TELEPHONE MESSAGE
FOR *Mr. Barton* .....
ROOM ....
FROM ....
....
....
....

5.
TELEPHONE MESSAGE
FOR *Mr. Donaldson* ....
ROOM ....
FROM ....
....
....
....

3.
TELEPHONE MESSAGE
FOR *Mrs. Ericsson* .....
ROOM ....
FROM ....
....
....
....

6.
TELEPHONE MESSAGE
FOR *Mr. Schollmeyer* .
ROOM ....
FROM ....
....
....
....

Role Play 9 (Stage A)

Caller: (Greet the receptionist.)

Receptionist: (Return the caller's greeting.) Can I help you, _____ ?

Caller: Yes, I'd like to speak to _____ in room _____ .

Receptionist: | What is | your name, _____ ?
| Can I have |

Caller: _____ .

Receptionist: I'll see whether _____ is in | his | room.
| her |

Role Play 9 (Stage B)

Receptionist: I'm afraid _____ is not in _____ room.

Caller: D'you think | he | is in the hotel? |
          | she | has gone out? |

Receptionist: _____ key is still here, _____ . | Would you like me to |
                | Shall I |

page _____ for you?

Caller: Would you mind?

Receptionist: Not at all, _____ . *(Page the guest for the caller.)*

Reading

The International Business Travellers' Club

As a member of the International Business Travellers' Club you will receive the following privileges:—

* Guaranteed availability of a room on the Executive Floor Levels. (These rooms allow extra space for the Businessman or Businesswoman).

* Early access to your room may be arranged if required.

* Complimentary Suit Pressing. *Fill in the card in your room and attach it to your suit, then simply call the valet on extension 3. Valet Service Mon-Sat 7 a.m. – 7 p.m.*

* Complimentary Shoeshine. Your shoes will be collected and polished: *– From 7 p.m. – 7 a.m. (Ext. 7) Please contact the Night Porter who will arrange collection, cleaning and the return of your shoes. From 7 a.m. – 7 p.m. (Ext. 3) Please contact the Valet who will collect, clean and return your shoes. If the Valet is closed please contact the Hall Porter extension 7.*

* Should your stay at the Royal Lancaster be unexpected, the Housekeeper and Duty Manager hold a supply of toiletries and hair dryers which are available on request via the Hotel Switchboard.

* Privilege of access to "The International Business Travellers' Club" Suite – located on the 14th Floor. Entry is gained by using the suite key 1427 provided with your room key. The suite comprises a lounge for both social and business meetings, and a separate office in which there are:–

    Colour Television; Teletext Business Information Centre; Radio and Cassette Recorder; Daily and Weekly Newspapers and Periodicals.

Should you use the suite please advise the Hotel Switchboard and Enquiry Desk to enable them to redirect messages and telephone calls.

Listening

Which messages fit the conversations? Fill in the missing details.

A

TELEPHONE MESSAGE
FOR . . . .
ROOM . . . .
FROM *Mr. Yasuka . . . .*
Mt. me. a.s.a.p. . . . . .
office. civic. centre . . . .
. . . .

B

TELEPHONE MESSAGE
FOR . . . .
ROOM . . . .
FROM *ARAMCO . . . . .*
Urg. mtng. Dhahran . .
off. Dec. 29 . . . .
Pls. return. a.s.a.p. . . .

C

TELEPHONE MESSAGE
FOR . . . .
ROOM . . . .
FROM *Brit. Emb. . . . . . .*
Tlx. rcvd. from. yr. .
family. Tel. Emb . . . .
urg. 82666. Ext. 9 . .

D

TELEPHONE MESSAGE
FOR . . . .
ROOM . . . .
FROM *Mr. Blair . . . . . .*
Pls. tel. Inter.-Conti. .
Rm. 886. urg. . . . .
. . . .

Listening

Which part of the hotel are these guests talking about?

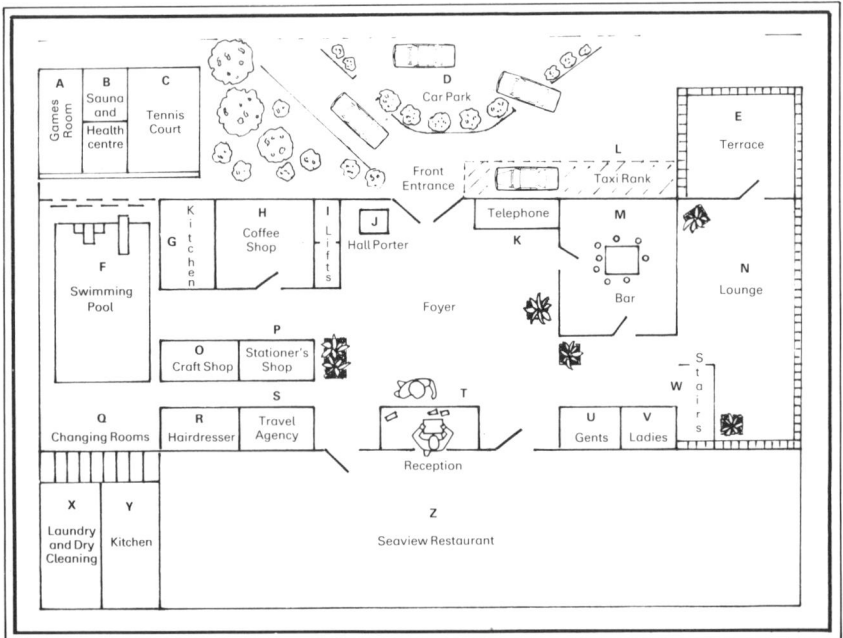

Role Play 9 (Alternative Stage B)

Guest: Hello, _____ speaking.

Receptionist: A | Mr | _____ has called to see you.
         | Mrs |
         | Miss |

Guest: Thank you. | Would you | tell _____
         | Please |

| to come straight up to my room. |
| to wait for me in the bar. |
| that I'll be down in a few minutes. |
| that I can't see _____ now. I'll phone _____ later. |

Receptionist: _____ | asks you to | _____ .
           | says that |

Caller: I see. Thank you.

Oral Work

1.  2.  3.  4.  5.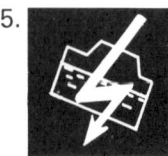

Listening

Where do these guests want to go?

A Post Office

B Ladies' Dress Shop

C Shoe Shop

D Flying Carpet Night Club

E Peacock Restaurant

F Newsagent/ Stationer's

G Dentist's Surgery

H Jeweller's

I Supermarket

J Furniture Shop

K Doctor's Surgery

L Exchange Bureau

M Immigration Office

Role Play 10 (Stage A)

Clerk: Hello, this is Reservations.

Caller: (Ask to reserve a room.)

Clerk: Certainly, _____ . For what dates?

Caller: (Give the dates.)

Clerk: So, that's _____ room(s) from (Repeat the dates you were given.)

Reading

Disabled Facilities:	Wheelchair access is possible to all public rooms. Corner bedrooms, with greater manoeuvering space for wheelchairs are allocated for disabled guests. A uni-sex disabled bathroom and toilet is located on the first floor opposite the Somerset Suite, accessible by lift from all floors.

Dogs:	Guide dogs are permitted.

Reading

DIRECTORY OF SERVICES

INFORMATION
Information will profide you address or phone number of the Government Office or any other office.
Information clerk are eager to answer all your questions regarding, services, air lines, shopping, sight seeing etc.

ROOM REGULATION
No visitor of the opposite sex are premitted to the room of registered guests after 20.00 p.m.
In all cases; each visit must be announced to the front office, and the guest room door should be left open during the visit.

ELECTRICITY
Use of any other electrical appliances in your room is expressly forbidden, except for electric razor using.

DRESS
Usually informil. Guest should appropriately dressed esp for ladies.
Bathing suites or shorts are suitable only in the guest room.

LAUNDRY
Laundry facilities are served by Housekeeping. Regular service takes in less than two days. Special service at an extra charge is available if the items are received before 02.00 p.m.
You are requested to note down on the laundry list which is prepared in your room.
Only a room boy should receive and deliver your laundry.

OTHER SERVICES
The room-boy will always be happy to polish your shoes free of charge.
Taxi are available through the help of the front office clerk but please make your reservation a head of time.
Should you wish to charge the fare to your hotel account, kindly sign the slip.

Role Play 10 (Stage B)

Clerk: (Ask for the caller's name.)

Caller: (Give your name.)

Clerk: (Repeat the name, checking the spelling if necessary.)

Caller: (Correct any mistakes the caller makes.)

Listening

What are these guests complaining about? Write their room numbers beside the person you should report the fault to.

Report fault to	Room numbers
A Electrician	
B Plumber	
C Housekeeper	
D Room Service	
E Head Barman	
F Chief Accountant	
G Food & Beverage Manager	

Listening

Are these guests satisfied or dissatisfied?

1.
4.
7.

2.
5.
8.

3.
6.
9.

Role Play 10 (Stage C)

Clerk: Could you write and confirm that reservation, _____ ?

Caller: Yes, I'll write tomorrow. But I haven't got the proper address of your hotel. Could you give it to me?

Clerk: Yes, our address is *(Give the address slowly so the caller can write it down. Offer to spell it.)*

Caller: Let me see if I've got that. *(Repeat the address.)*

Clerk: *(Correct any mistakes the caller makes.)*

Reading

HOW TO PROCESS CHARGES

(a) Imprint, or copy details of the card onto a Carte Blanche charge voucher. Include the amount of the transaction and date of the charge.

(b) Be sure the amount of the sale is within your specified credit limit. *

NOTE: If your establishment receives the Carte Blanche warning notice, check that the card number is not listed on the current copy.

(c) Request the cardholder to sign the voucher in the space provided and compare the signature with that in the signature panel on the Carte Blanche card.

(d) Give the bottom (cardholder) copy of the voucher to the cardholder. Retain the top (establishment) copy in your files for one year. Send the hard, white (Carte Blanche) copy to Carte Blanche within ten days, along with all other charges received in the ten day period, accompanied by a complete summary card.

Listening

What do you think these guests want?

1. This guest wants to know:
   - (a) how to call room service.
   - (b) where the lifts are.
   - (c) if he can reserve a room.

2. This guest wants you to:
   - (a) give her change of 10 dinars.
   - (b) pay the taxi driver for her.
   - (c) argue about the fare with the driver.

3. This guest:
   - (a) is leaving and wants his bill.
   - (b) wants to know where the restaurant is.
   - (c) is sick and needs some medicine.

4. This guest wants:
   - (a) the porter.
   - (b) to find the lifts.
   - (c) an early morning call.

5. This guest is complaining about:
   - (a) the heat.
   - (b) the bill.
   - (c) the price.

6. This guest is complaining:
   - (a) about the drycleaning service.
   - (b) that there is no water.
   - (c) that her room has not been cleaned.

7. This guest wants:
   - (a) a knife.
   - (b) the police.
   - (c) a haircut.

8. This guest wants:
   - (a) you to speak a bit louder.
   - (b) to know if you paged him.
   - (c) to leave a message for a caller.

Role Play 11 (Stage A)

Guest: (Ask for help at the desk.)

Receptionist: (Show your willingness to help.)

Guest: (Ask the receptionist to recommend a restaurant where you can have some special food.)

Receptionist: (From your knowledge of your own town, recommend the kind of restaurant the guest wants.)

Guest: (Ask whereabouts the restaurant is.)

Receptionist: (Answer, but just giving rough directions – e.g. it's near _____.)

Oral work

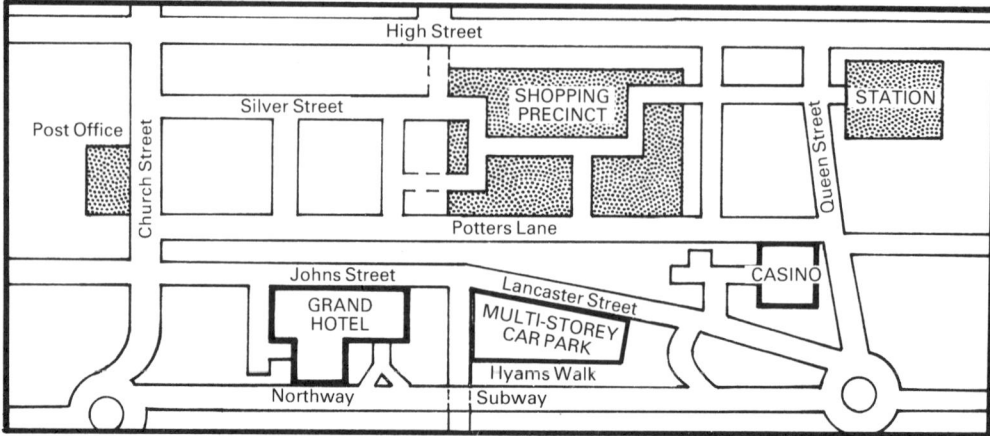

Oral Work

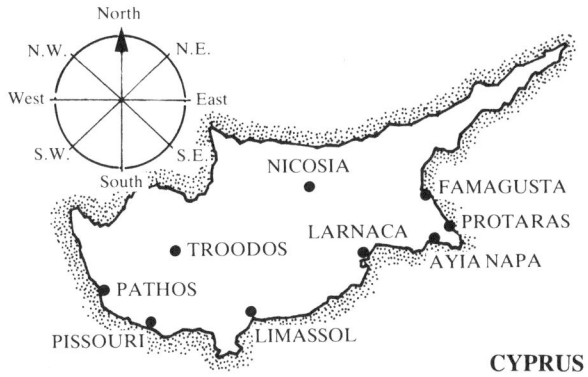

CYPRUS

Role Play 11 (Stage B)

Guest: *(Ask if it's near or far from the hotel.)*

Receptionist: *(Say it's too far to walk and advise taking a taxi.)*

Guest: *(Ask the receptionist to write down the name, and ask how much you should pay for the taxi, roughly.)*

(Alternative Stage B)

Guest: *(Ask if it's near or far from the hotel.)*

Receptionist: *(Say it's very near and, using the map, give directions for getting there.)*

Listening

Are these guests asking a question or making a statement?

	Question	Statement
Guest No. 1		
Guest No. 2		
Guest No. 3		
Guest No. 4		
Guest No. 5		
Guest No. 6		
Guest No. 7		
Guest No. 8		
Guest No. 9		

38

Role Play 12 (Stage A)

Guest: *(Tell the receptionist that you have a problem and ask for help.)*

Receptionist: *(Express your willingness to help.)*

Guest: *(Explain that you have lost something important – e.g. a briefcase, or your passport.)*

Receptionist: *(Ask the guest when he/she last remembers seeing it.)*

Guest: *(Say you had it when you left the hotel this morning.)*

Listening

What do these guests want?

1. This guest:
   - (a) is going and wants to check out.
   - (b) has lost something from his room.
   - (c) wants to borrow the master key.

2. This guest:
   - (a) wants you to lend him a pen.
   - (b) is enquiring about a lost pen.
   - (c) took your pen away by mistake.

3. This guest wants to know:
   - (a) if she can have Mr Johnson's key.
   - (b) if Mr Johnson is in the hotel.
   - (c) what Mr Johnson's room number is.

4. This guest wants:
   - (a) to get his washing back.
   - (b) to buy some new shirts.
   - (c) the phone number of the laundry.

5. This guest wants:
   - (a) directions to a place.
   - (b) you to attend to him.
   - (c) to wait a bit longer.

6. This guest:
   - (a) doesn't understand what you're saying.
   - (b) wants to confirm her reservation.
   - (c) is angry there is no reservation for her.

7. This guest wants information about:
   - (a) a famous Roman.
   - (b) part of the city.
   - (c) a historic place.

8. This guest:
   - (a) wants you to recommend a shop.
   - (b) is telling you about his wife.
   - (c) is asking about the price of gold.

Reading

JOB DESCRIPTION

POSITION: RECEPTIONIST   DEPARTMENT: FRONT OFFICE

1. Welcoming and registering clients.
2. Helping them with any queries or problems that arise.
3. The answering of all telephones quickly and efficiently.
4. The taking of reservations, cancellations and revisions.
5. Manning the Advance Reservations department between 5.30 p.m. and 9.30 a.m.
6. The sending, receiving and distribution of telexes and cables.
7. The typing of all guests' folios, and the distribution of Whitney Slips.
8. Carrying out other duties as directed by the Chef de Brigade. This also entails special guest services.
9. Handling and registration of large groups and conferences.
10. Selling Hotel at maximum % coupled with maximum room rate.

Listening

What is the best thing to say in reply?

1. (a) Good night, sir.
   (b) Good evening.
   (c) Hello, sir.

2. (a) Say your name again, lady.
   (b) Could you repeat your name, please.
   (c) Please speak more clearly, madam.

3. (a) Can I help you, Mr Webb?
   (b) Nice to meet you, Mr Webb.
   (c) What do you want, Mr Webb?

4. (a) Wait a moment, Miss, while I check.
   (b) I'll have to look at the list, madam.
   (c) I won't keep you a moment, Mrs Scott.

5. (a) Certainly.
   (b) O.K.
   (c) I've checked.

6. (a) No, you didn't.
   (b) I'll check the list again.
   (c) You can have 2 singles.

7. (a) I'm sorry for the delay, sir.
   (b) We're very busy, sir.
   (c) Just a moment, sir.

8. (a) Here you are, madam.
   (b) O.K.
   (c) I haven't got one.

9. (a) I'll call a porter.
   (b) You want a porter?
   (c) The porter's over there.

10. (a) Maybe it's possible.
    (b) The showers are very good.
    (c) I'll see what I can do.

Role Play 12 (Stage B)

Guest: *(Say you were visiting a customer's office all morning, then returned to the hotel by taxi.)*

Receptionist: *(Ask if he/she has contacted the customer to see if he/she left it in the office.)*

Guest: *(Explain that you can't find that out because the customer has now left the office and there is no one else there who speaks English.)*

Receptionist: *(Offer to phone the office to find out if it's there.)*

Guest: *(Express your gratitude to the receptionist.)*

Receptionist: *(Ask the guest to give you the office telephone number.)*

Guest: *(Give a number.)*

Oral Work

40

Role Play 12 (Stage C)

Receptionist: (Tell the guest they have not seen it in their office.)

Guest: (Tell the receptionist you must have lost it in the taxi.)

Receptionist: (Ask the guest how he/she got the taxi. Did the office call it?)

Guest: (Say you got a passing taxi in the street.)

Receptionist: (Explain that it might be difficult to trace (i.e. find) the taxi. Offer to notify the police.)

Guest: (Thank the receptionist for helping you.)

Listening

What do these guests want?

1. This guest:
   - (a) is complaining about people banging loudly on his door.
   - (b) says the lift keeps passing the second floor.
   - (c) thinks there are people in the lift who can't get out.

2. This guest wants:
   - (a) you to recommend a shoe shop.
   - (b) to know if she can walk to the shops.
   - (c) you to call a taxi for her.

3. This guest is worried because:
   - (a) there has been a mix-up with the rooms.
   - (b) he doesn't know where the Browns are.
   - (c) the porter has brought the wrong cases.

4. This guest is worried because:
   - (a) she needs a doctor for her feet.
   - (b) she wants to buy some shoes.
   - (c) her shoes have been stolen.

5. This guest wants to know:
   - (a) where he can buy a magazine.
   - (b) what time the newsagents open.
   - (c) if the hotel sells foreign papers.

6. This guest:
   - (a) has fallen and hurt himself and needs help.
   - (b) is complaining about the dirt outside the hotel.
   - (c) wants to give you a box that he found outside.

7. This guest:
   - (a) is complaining about the wardrobe in his room.
   - (b) wants something to keep his broken case closed.
   - (c) wants you to help him tie up a parcel.

8. This guest is worried because he has lost:
   - (a) his newspapers.
   - (b) a small case.
   - (c) his telephone connection.

41

Listening

What is the best reply?

1. (a) Good morning.
   (b) Good afternoon.
   (c) Good evening.

2. (a) I hope you have a reservation, Miss.
   (b) Have you booked a room, madam.
   (c) The hotel is full unless you have a reservation.

3. (a) Good afternoon, I'm Samir.
   (b) Good afternoon Mr Hanson.
   (c) How do you do?

4. (a) Could you repeat your name, please?
   (b) Good evening. What's your name?
   (c) Say your name again, madam.

5. (a) Have you got a reservation?
   (b) Good morning, Mr Duval. Can I help you?
   (c) Good morning, sir. What do you want?

6. (a) This is a very big group, sir.
   (b) We're working as fast as we can, sir.
   (c) I'm sorry about the delay, sir.

7. (a) I'm afraid we don't, sir.
   (b) Certainly not, sir.
   (c) You must pay in cash, sir.

8. (a) What do you want?
   (b) Certainly, if I can.
   (c) O.K. I'll help.

9. (a) Repeat that spelling for me.
   (b) Could you spell that again?
   (c) Say that one more time.

10. (a) I'm very sorry, sir, we don't accept Diners Cards.
    (b) We only accept American Express in this hotel.
    (c) Diners Cards are not acceptable here, sir.

Reading

Amman, a modern capital, is the gateway to Jordan's legendary cities of the past. For thousands of years this city, near the fertile Jordan valley, was the crossroads for people of many nations. Today, Amman continues to welcome countless visitors.

Excellent roads make exploration of this small and friendly country easy. Less than an hour's drive to the north is Jerash . . . the jewel of Greco-Roman cities. To the south, three hours by car then half an hour on horseback, discover Petra, a city carved out of rose red rock 2,000 years ago and 'lost' for centuries.

There are desert castles, biblical battlegrounds, walled cities and ancient churches all within easy driving distance. The palm lined beaches and crystal waters of Aqaba, Jordan's resort on the Red Sea, are a mere 45 minutes' flight away.

Role Play 13 (Stage A)

Receptionist: (Greet the guest and ask if you can help.)

Guest: (Explain that you have a free day on Friday and you would like to see a bit of the country. Ask where you can hire a car for the day.)

Receptionist: (Tell the guest where to hire a car.)

Guest: (Ask if the receptionist knows the cost of a day's hire.)

Receptionist: (Give an idea of the cost, if you can. If you can't, apologise.)

Listening

What would you say to these guests?

1. (a) I'm sorry, madam, the guest in 405 is not in.
   (b) I'm afraid not. Would you like to take the master key?
   (c) Can't you remember where you had it last?

2. (a) Don't worry, sir, you'll get them all back eventually.
   (b) I'm sorry to hear that, sir. I'll notify the police at once.
   (c) I'm sorry, sir. I'll pass your complaint on to the housekeeper.

3. (a) It's too far for an old man like you. Take a taxi.
   (b) Perhaps you should take a taxi. It's quite a long way.
   (c) Walk there? You must be mad!

4. (a) Don't worry. We <u>will</u> post it.
   (b) Of course we'll post it.
   (c) I'd advise you to go to the Post Office.

5. (a) I'm sorry, sir. I'll cancel your order.
   (b) I'll give that message to your friends, sir.
   (c) I'll have the drinks sent to your room, sir.

6. (a) If you are not satisfied, you can go to a bank.
   (b) The exchange rates can change from day to day.
   (c) I'm afraid we have to add a charge for this service.

7. (a) I'll see that you are not bothered, madam.
   (b) I'll pass that message on to any callers, madam.
   (c) I'm sorry the call was not put through to you, madam.

8. (a) I'm sorry, that's the only map we have.
   (b) Perhaps I can help you. Where do you want to go?
   (c) Amman is confusing at first, but you soon find your way around.

Reading

DEAR GUEST!

To help you enjoy your stay, every room has been provided with a bathrobe.

Please leave the robe in your room after use. Your room attendant has signed out for a definite number and is responsible for it.

If you wish to buy a robe, please inform the front office cashier who will charge your account.

Your cooperation is appreciated and we thank you.

43

Listening

What do these guests want?

1. This guest is worried because he:
   - (a) was expecting someone to call.
   - (b) hasn't received a letter.
   - (c) can't get transport to the bank.

2. This guest wants:
   - (a) to cancel his breakfast order.
   - (b) to order breakfast quickly.
   - (c) breakfast in an hour's time.

3. This guest wants:
   - (a) to leave his luggage with you.
   - (b) you to call a porter.
   - (c) to report a missing case.

4. This guest wants:
   - (a) to know what time it is.
   - (b) directions to the Civic Centre.
   - (c) to find the taxi-rank.

5. This guest is asking about:
   - (a) climate differences.
   - (b) electricity cuts.
   - (c) exchange rates.

6. This guest is giving you some jewellery:
   - (a) that someone has lost.
   - (b) to put in the hotel safe.
   - (c) to keep as a present.

7. This guest wants:
   - (a) to know where the swimming pool is.
   - (b) to report he lost a ring at the pool.
   - (c) you to page his wife at the pool.

8. This guest:
   - (a) is complaining about Jordanian food.
   - (b) wants you to recommend a restaurant.
   - (c) wants information about tours in Jordan.

9. This guest wants:
   - (a) to have his nails cut.
   - (b) to have his shoes repaired.
   - (c) to complain about the food.

10. This guest needs:
    - (a) a dentist.
    - (b) a doctor.
    - (c) a chemist.

Role Play 13 (Stage B)

Guest: (Ask the receptionist to recommend an interesting place to visit.)

Receptionist: (Suggest two interesting places.)

Guest: (Ask the receptionist to tell you more about the first place he/she mentioned.)

Receptionist: (Give the guest as much information as possible about the (historical) interest of the first place you suggested.)

Guest: (Ask how far it is.)

Receptionist: (Answer the question.)

Oral Work

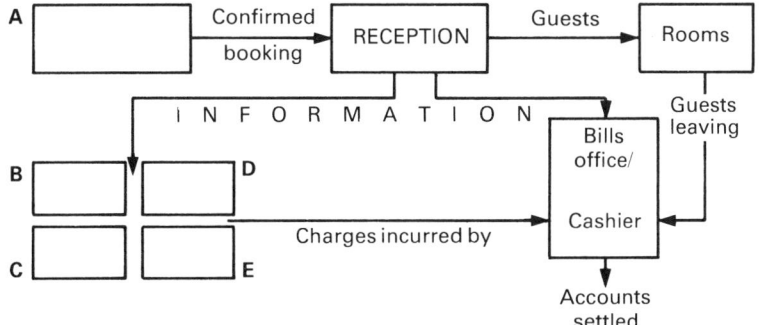

Role Play 13 (Stage C)

Guest: *(Ask the receptionist to tell you more about the second place mentioned.)*

Receptionist: *(Give the guest as much information as you can about the (historical) interest of the second place.)*

Guest: *(Ask how far it is.)*

Receptionist: *(Answer the question.)*

Guest: *(Say which place you have decided to go to.)*

Receptionist: *(Wish the guest a good trip.)*

Listening

Listen to the directions the receptionist gives and decide where the rooms are.

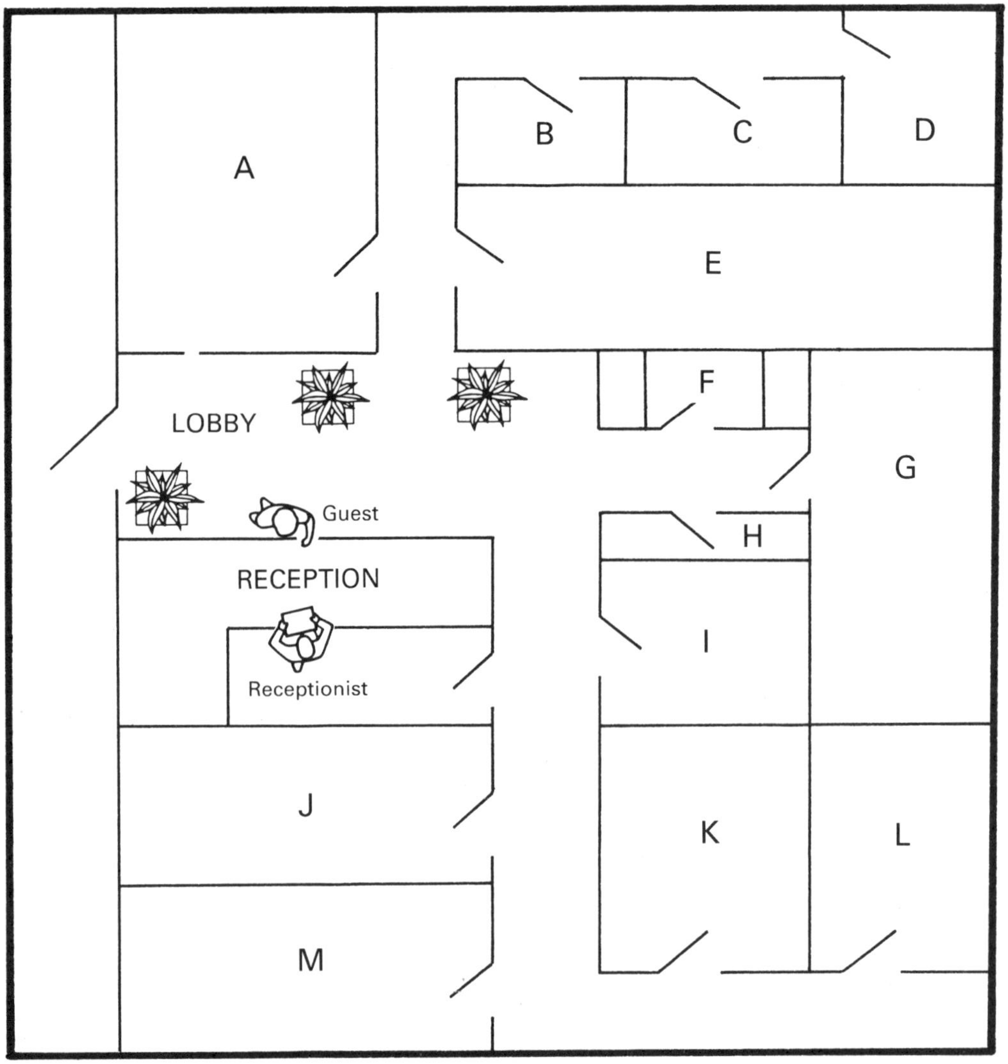

A

B   C   D

E

F

G

LOBBY

H

Guest

I

RECEPTION

Receptionist

J

K   L

M

45

Listening

Write down the names and addresses.

1. Name   _____

    Address   _____

                 _____

                 _____

2. Name   _____

    Address   _____

                 _____

                 _____

3. Name   _____

    Address   _____

                 _____

                 _____

4. Name   _____

    Address   _____

                 _____

                 _____

5. Name   _____

    Address   _____

                 _____

                 _____

Reading

Assistant Manager *(Hotel)*

To assist the General Manager in all aspects of the hotel's operation and to assume control in his absence.

The successful applicants are most likely to:
- Be 23-30 years of age
- Be single or married without children
- Have completed their Diploma Course and have at least two years further practical experience
- Hold current driving licence
- Be available to assume duties by October

We are offering
- 2 year contracts
- Round trip air fares
- Accommodation with full board
- Salary commensurate with age and experience – payable in US dollars (Income Tax 7%)
- Three weeks' annual paid vacation

Applications in writing giving full details of education, experience and interests to:

Box No. 1079

Applicants selected for interview will be advised by telephone. Please give telephone contact number. All replies will be treated in strict confidence.

Reading

Today's hotel thief is prosperous

IN A hotel in the German city of Hanover thieves cleared an entire room. Their haul included bedlinen, a standard lamp and a carpet. And the room is on the sixth floor!

In Hamburg a guest took the television set provided in his room and packed it up in a cardboard box. He then had it removed from the premises by a helpful and unsuspecting member of the hotel staff.

Not all hotel thefts have that degree of panache. The massive amount of money that hotels lose through theft dribbles away bit by bit as thousands of guests check out with small items of property in their luggage — ashtrays, towels, coathangers, spoons, salt cellars, writing cases, and other easily portable objects.

To give some idea of the scale of the hotel theft problem, according to the West German economics weekly *Wirtschaftswoche*; the Düsseldorf Hilton reckons that half of all its replacement purchases each year are due to theft; the "shopping list" includes 1,500 bath towels, 500 bath mats, 6,000 coathangers, 240 silver coffee spoons, 2,800 china ashtrays, 1,200 glass ashtrays, 1,500 salt cellars and pepper pots, and 400 leather writing cases.

The problem is so troublesome that a former Munich police psychologist, now a management consultant, decided to question a number of people who had stolen articles from hotels about their motives. He identified three distinct types of offenders.

The souvenir thief, as one would expect, prefers objects that carry the name or the crest of the hotel. What this offender is stealing is the proof that he, or she, has stayed in a particular place. People in this category, according to the psychologist, want something of the hotel's prestige to rub off on them. Naturally, they usually report themselves satisfied with the hotel concerned.

It is different with the second type, the revenge thief. This offender steals something because he wants to punish the hotel for some defect in the service he has received. He may help himself to a bath towel or a picture. Or he may drink a bottle of Champagne from the fridge, re-fill the bottle with water, and replace the silver paper carefully on the top of the bottle.

The third type of offender simply wants to stock up with items which will be useful for his own home. A favourite form of loot for this type of thief has been the portable television set, but some hoteliers have done something to lessen this problem by installing larger sets in guests' rooms.

The new type of hotel thief is likely to be a prosperous businessman travelling for his firm. Psychologists believe that this type of offender is often reacting against the stresses and strains of life. A large hotel represents a refuge from normal life. It offers an atmosphere of anonymity and operates as a kind of safety valve for society. And so guests feel free to behave in a more unrestrained way than is possible in their normal environment.

To a certain extent, the attitude of hotel managers is, and has to be, one of resignation. One manager pointed out that it is possible for staff to carry out a quick inventory of a room while a guest is checking out. In this way an offender can be intercepted in the hotel lobby and quietly taken on one side.

But, as this manager said, "when all's said and done we don't want to antagonise our customers".

Consequently, many people in the hotel industry are resigned to the do-nothing policy. Some feel that the cost of effective security would be higher than the cost of replacing stolen articles, which is budgeted for anyway.

Many hotels have taken to equipping their rooms more cheaply, with plastic replacing leather or china. Some items, such as pictures and lamps, can be screwed into place.

One hotelier continues to hang pictures on nails, but with a red sign fixed to the wall behind each picture reading "Missing". The psychological effect of this stratagem is said to be impressive – there are no more problems as far as pictures are concerned.

Role Play 14

This role play is not between a receptionist and a guest. The characters in this role play are the manager(s) of the hotel that placed the advertisement you read on the previous page, and one of the people who has applied for the job of Assistant Manager.

Interviewers should ask the applicant questions about his/her school education, hotel training qualifications, work experience, how soon he/she could start a new job.

Applicants should ask the interviewers about the hotel, the living accommodation, the salary and the country.

Reference section

Hotel Terms

adjoining rooms	rooms next to each other
advance reservation	a reservation made in advance, i.e. before arrival – recorded on the **advance reservations chart**
alphabetical guest index	(also known as 'A to Z') a list of names of all the hotel guests, arranged in alphabetical order
American plan	accommodation and 3 meals a day (same as **full board** and **en pension**)
arrival and departure list	a sheet showing names of arriving guests in one column and departing guests in another, updated daily
available	ready for use, e.g. 'I'm afraid we have no single rooms available at the moment.'
banquet	large, formal dinner – often held in a banqueting room
bed booking chart	(see **advance reservations chart**)
bed occupancy list	a list compiled by the housekeeper showing which rooms are occupied and by how many people (same as **room status report**)
black list	a confidential list of people who are not welcome at the hotel (see page 13)
block booking	a booking made for a number of people at the same time and for the same period
booking	reservation
cancel	to say that you no longer want to keep an arrangement, e.g. 'Mr and Mrs Jones have cancelled their reservation for next week.'
cancellation	(see **cancel**) e.g. 'If we don't get any cancellations we'll be fully booked next week.'
cashier	an employee who deals with money, e.g. 'The cashier will prepare your bill at once, sir.'
chance bookings/guests/trade	guests who arrive without a reservation, e.g. 'Because the hotel is so near the station, we get a lot of chance trade.'
charge (1)	(v.) to make someone pay for something (n.) an amount to be paid for goods or services e.g. 'We don't charge guests for local telephone calls, but we do make a charge for long-distance ones.' 'The guests in 104 have incurred no charges for the minibar.'
charge (2)	to put something on an account rather than pay cash for it, e.g. 'Please charge Mr Brown's bill to our company.'
check in	to arrive and register at a hotel, e.g. 'Has a Mr Green checked in yet?'
check out	to pay the bill and leave a hotel
chef de brigade	the person in charge of the reception staff
client	a customer, a guest in the hotel

communicating rooms	rooms that are next to one another and have a door between them so that guests can go from one to the other without using the corridor
complaint	saying you are dissatisfied with something, e.g. 'I'd like to make a complaint about the waiter who served me at lunch.'
complimentary	given free out of kindness or respect, e.g. 'All our guests receive a complimentary bowl of fruit in their rooms when they check in.' (same as **courtesy**)
compliments	as in 'with the compliments of . . .', a phrase used when giving the name of the person offering a gift, e.g. 'These flowers are with the compliments of the management.'
concierge	(see **porter**)
conference room	a large room suitable for meetings
confirm	to say that an arrangement is definite, e.g. 'Please confirm your reservation in writing.'
confirmation	(see **confirm**) e.g. 'We haven't received confirmation of that booking.'
continuation bill	a second sheet added to a guest's bill when the first sheet is full
convenient	useful for one's needs, e.g. 'The hotel is in a very convenient position in the town centre.'
courier	tour leader, employed by a hotel or travel agency
courtesy	(see **complimentary**) e.g. 'Our hotel runs a courtesy bus service to and from the airport.'
currency	the particular type of money of a country, e.g. 'Foreign currency may be changed at the cashier's office.'
date of birth	the day, month and year when someone was born (N.B. not 'birthday') e.g. 'My date of birth is the 4th of October 1951.' 'My birthday is the 4th of October.'
debtor	someone who owes money
debtor's ledger	(see **ledger**)
demi-pension	room, breakfast and one other meal, e.g. 'We've booked you at the demi-pension rate.' (same as **half board**)
departure list	a list produced each day of guests who will be checking out of the hotel that day
deposit (1)	(*v.*) to leave something for safe keeping, e.g. 'Please deposit all valuables with the front office.'
deposit (2)	(*n.*) a sum of money paid in advance and then subtracted from the account, e.g. 'The tour operators ask for a deposit of $100 when you confirm your booking.'
directory	a book that lists names in alphabetical order, e.g. 'You will find their number in the telephone directory.'
discount	a **reduction** in price, e.g. 'Our company uses that hotel a lot, so they give us a 10% discount.'
doorman	(see **porter**)
double room	a room for 2 people, either with twin beds or with a double bed
early morning call sheet	a sheet of paper on which the receptionist notes what time guests want an early call, and whether they want tea and/or newspapers

electrician	a person who looks after the electrical fittings in a building, e.g. 'I'll get the electrician to repair the air conditioning in your room.'
en pension	(see **American plan**)
escalator	a moving staircase
European plan	accommodation only, with no meals, e.g. 'The European plan is more popular with our business clients.'
exchange rate	the value of one currency compared to another, e.g. 'What is today's exchange rate for the dollar?'
excursion	local trip to places of interest or beauty, e.g. 'Would you like to join our excursion to Lake Windermere this afternoon?'
facilities	space and equipment that make it possible for guests to do certain things, e.g. sports facilities, conference facilities, laundry facilities
float	an amount of money given to a member of staff for the purpose of giving change, e.g. 'We give the barman a float of £10 in small change.'
form	a piece of printed paper with space in which to write information, e.g. 'All guests must fill in a registration form when they check in.'
foyer	the front hall of a hotel, e.g. 'I'll meet you in the foyer at six.' (same as **lobby**)
free of charge	not costing anything (see also **charge** and **complimentary**)
full board	(see **American plan**)
full price	the advertised price with no reductions, e.g. 'We offer long-stay guests a discount, but short-stay guests are charged the full price.'
fully booked	having no vacancies, e.g. 'I'm sorry we can't reserve a room for tomorrow night for you. The hotel is fully booked.'
guaranteed booking	a definite booking for which the guest will be charged even if he/she does not arrive
half board	(see **demi-pension**)
handyman	someone who does general repair and maintenance work, e.g. 'I'll get the handyman to mend the broken chair.'
high season	the most popular and busiest time of year e.g. 'In Portuguese resorts the high season is from June to September.' (same as **peak season**)
hotel chain	a number of hotels, often in different countries, owned by one company, e.g. 'The Hilton hotel chain has a hotel in most capital cities.'
hotel register	a book used to record guests' names, addresses, etc., which the guests sign on arrival (see also **register**)
identification	way of proving who you are, e.g. 'We can't change your travellers cheques without some form of identification. Your passport or driving licence will do.'
inclusive terms	the rate charged for accommodation and all meals, e.g. 'He would like to know what we charge for room only, and what our inclusive terms are.'
in house	booked in the hotel at that time, e.g. 'Can you tell me if Mr James Walker is in house?'

initial	the first letter of a name, e.g. 'I can't make out these initials – are they J.M. or J.N.?'
international hotel code	a code used all over the world for reserving hotel accommodation
itinerary	list of places to be visited, plan of a journey
key card	a card given to guests when they register showing the room number and rate, and sometimes describing the hotel's services (see page 10)
laundry (1)	the place where clothes are washed or dry cleaned
laundry (2)	dirty clothes to be washed or which have been washed, e.g. 'Laundry left for collection before 10 a.m. will be returned the same day.
lavatory	toilet
ledger	a book for recording money transactions, e.g. debtors' ledger, outstanding accounts ledger, sales ledger
linkman	(see **porter**)
lobby	(see **foyer**)
local call	a telephone call within a town or small area
long-distance call	a telephone call which is neither local nor international
lounge bar	bar with comfortable seats
low season	the least popular and quietest time of the year, e.g. 'From January to April, in the low season, we reduce our prices to try and attract guests.' (same as **off season**)
luggage	suitcases and bags, e.g. 'All your luggage is in the taxi, madam.'
luggage book	a book which the porter or luggage master uses to record the movement of luggage inside the hotel
luggage master	the person who controls the luggage porters
luggage pass	a card that shows permission for a guest's luggage to leave the hotel, indicating that the account has been settled
mini bar	a small refrigerator filled with drinks in a guest's room
non-arrival	a guest who has a reservation but does not arrive, e.g. 'One of yesterday's non-arrivals has phoned to say her plane was delayed and she's arriving today.' (same as **no show**)
no show	(see **non-arrival**)
off	not available for letting for some reason such as redecorating, e.g. 'Rooms 103 to 7 are off this week.'
off season	(see **low season**)
ooo	written abbreviation for Out of Order, i.e. not working
operator	a person who works with a certain machine, e.g. a telephone operator, telex operator, lift operator (see also **tour operator**)
outstanding	not yet paid
package tour	fixed price holiday for which the travel and accommodation are arranged by a company and which the customer pays for in advance
page boy	(see **porter**)
parcels books	a book used to record all parcels delivered to the hotel for guests

person to person call	a telephone call made through the operator, where the caller names the person he/she wants to speak to
porter	porters have different titles and duties depending on the size of the hotel: the **head porter** supervises the other porters hall porters deal with guests' enquiries and requests and, in a small hotel, with luggage **luggage porters** are hall porters who deal only with luggage the **concierge** is a hall porter who gives out and receives room keys the **linkman** or **doorman,** at a large hotel, opens car and taxi doors and escorts guests the **page boy** escorts guests within the hotel, e.g. shows them to their rooms
pre-registered booking	a booking that is held and charged from the previous night to allow guests early access to the room the following morning
prescription	piece of paper written by a doctor, used to obtain medicine
rate	usual charge, e.g. 'The rate for a room with bath is higher than the rate for a room with shower.'
rack rate	full room rate with no reduction (see **rate**)
receipt	a signed statement that money or something valuable has been received
reduction	(see **discount**)
referral	passing a client on to another hotel when you are fully booked, e.g. 'Three of our guests are referrals from the Plaza.'
register	to enter one's name in the hotel register or fill in a registration card
room board	(see **room status board**)
room service	delivery of food and drinks to a guest's room, e.g. 'Dial 3 for room service, madam.'
room status	the condition and availability of a room – whether it is occupied, ready for letting, in need of repairs or redecoration, e.g. 'What's the room status of 1204?'
room status board	board showing room status (same as **room board**)
room status report	(see **bed occupancy list**)
safe	a lockable metal cupboard where money and valuables can be kept safely
safe deposit box	one of a set of individual lockable boxes that guests can use to keep their valuables in
shannon	small piece of coloured card on which booking details are recorded (see **Whitney system**)
six p.m. release	booking where the room is not held after 6 p.m. unless the guest advises the hotel of late arrival
standby flight/ticket	airline flight or ticket obtained by the traveller at short notice, i.e. just before departure
stationery	writing paper and envelopes, e.g. 'Stationery is provided in the lounge as well as in guests' rooms.'
stock card	card giving details (e.g. beds, rate) of a hotel room

surcharge	extra charge
tour operator	travel company which operates **package tours**
vacant	empty, available for use
vacancies	empty rooms, e.g. 'I'm sorry, sir, we're fully booked at the moment. We have no vacancies until next week.'
V.I.P.	abbreviation for 'Very Important Person', e.g. 'We have 3 V.I.P.s arriving today.'
voucher	kind of ticket that can be used instead of money, e.g. presented by a guest who has already paid an agent for his/her room
Whitney system	a system for recording reservations in which coloured cards **(shannons)** are displayed in metal racks in alphabetical order (for a detailed explanation of this and other terms, see White & Beckley, *Hotel Reception,* pub. Edward Arnold)

American Terms

Some American English terms and their British English equivalents or meanings

U.S. Term	Meaning or U.K. Equivalent
baggage, luggage	luggage
bartender	barman
bathroom, restroom, washroom	toilet
bell boy, bell hop, page	page boy
bill	note (paper money) e.g. a dollar bill
bill fold	wallet
blank, form	form, e.g. a telegraph form
call collect	to make a reverse-charge call
candy	sweets
car hop	person who parks your car for you
check	a) bill for food b) US spelling of cheque
chef de brigade	head hall porter
chips	crisps
clerk, desk clerk	receptionist
closet	cupboard, wardrobe
comfort station	public toilet
cookie	biscuit
diaper	nappy
drapes	curtains
drug store	chemist's
elevator	lift
fall	autumn
fast food	food that is ready quickly, e.g. hamburgers, usually bought at a 'fast food restaurant'
faucet	tap
first floor	ground floor
folks	family
freeway	motorway
fries, French fries	chips, French fried potatoes
garbage, trash	rubbish
gas	petrol
gents' room	gents, gents' toilet
grip	travel bag, holdall
highway	main road
hood	bonnet (of a car)
icebox	fridge, refrigerator
information	directory enquiries (telephone)
junk food	food with low nutritive value. Often used to mean 'fast food'
ladies' room	ladies, ladies' toilet

mail	post
movie	film
movie house, movie theatre	cinema
overpass	flyover
outlet	power point (electric)
pants	trousers
pocket book	purse
purse	handbag
railroad	railway
sidewalk	pavement
sink	washbasin
store	shop
streetcar	tram
subway	underground, tube
trash can	dustbin
trunk	boot (of a car)
ZIP code	post code

National Profiles

A selective list of countries of the world with information of interest to the receptionist and others dealing with international travellers.

Country	Adjective	Official Language(s)	Capital	Unit of Currency	Main International Airline(s)
Algeria	Algerian	Arabic French	Algiers	Dinar	Air Algerie
Argentina	Argentinian (or Argentine)	Spanish	Buenos Aires	Peso	Aerolineas Argentinas
Australia	Australian	English	Canberra	Australian Dollar	Qantas
Austria	Austrian	German	Vienna	Schilling	Austrian Airlines
Bahamas	Bahamian	English	Nassau	Bahamian Dollar	Bahamas Air
Bahrain	Bahraini	Arabic	Manama	Bahraini Dinar	Gulf Air
Bangladesh	Bangladesh (person = [a] Bangladeshi	Bengali	Dacca	Taka	Biman
Barbados	Barbadian	English	Bridgetown	Barbados Dollar	Caribbean Airways
Belgium	Belgian	Flemish French	Brussels	Belgian Franc	Sabena
Bolivia	Bolivian	Spanish	La Paz	Peso	LAB (Lloyd Aereo Boliviano)
Brazil	Brazilian	Portuguese	Brasilia	Cruzeiro	Varig
Cameroon	Cameroonian	French English	Yaounde	Franc	Cameroon Airlines
Canada	Canadian	English French	Ottawa	Canadian Dollar	Air Canada Canadian Pacific Wardair
Chile	Chilean	Spanish	Santiago	Escudo	Lan-Chile
China	Chinese	Chinese, i.e. Cantonese, Mandarin	Beijing (Peking)	Yuan	China Airlines
Colombia	Colombian	Spanish	Bogota	Peso	Avianca
Cyprus	Cypriot	Greek Turkish	Nicosia	Cyprus Pound	Cyprus Airways
Denmark	Danish (person = a Dane)	Danish	Copenhagen	Krone	SAS (Scandinavian Airlines)
Ecuador	Ecuadorian	Spanish	Quito	Sucre	Equatoriana
Egypt	Egyptian	Arabic	Cairo	Egyptian Pound	Egyptair
England	English	English	London	Pound (Sterling)	British Airways British Caledonian

Country	Adjective	Official Language(s)	Capital	Unit of Currency	Main International Airline(s)
Finland	Finnish (person = a Finn)	Finnish Swedish	Helsinki	Markka	Finnair
France	French	French	Paris	Franc	Air France
The Gambia	Gambian	English	Banjul	Dalasi	—
Germany, West	German	German	Bonn	Mark	Lufthansa
Ghana	Ghanaian	English	Accra	Cedi	Ghana Airways
Great Britain – *see U.K.*					
Greece	Greek	Greek	Athens	Drachma	Olympic Airways
Hong Kong	Hong Kong (not person)	English Chinese, i.e. Cantonese	Victoria	Hong Kong Dollar	Cathay Pacific
Iceland	Icelandic	Icelandic	Reykjavik	Krona	Loftleidir (Icelandic Airlines)
India	Indian	Hindi English	Delhi	Rupee	Air India
Indonesia	Indonesian	Bahasa Indonesia English	Jakarta	Rupiah	Garuda Indonesia Airways
Iraq	Iraqi	Arabic	Baghdad	Iraqi Dinar	Iraqi Airways
Ireland (Eire)	Irish	English Gaelic	Dublin	Irish Pound	Aer Lingus
Ireland, Northern	Irish	English	Belfast	Pound (Sterling)	British Airways
Italy	Italian	Italian	Rome	Lira	Alitalia
Jamaica	Jamaican	English	Kingston	Jamaican Dollar	Air Jamaica
Japan	Japanese	Japanese	Tokyo	Yen	JAL (Japan Airlines)
Jordan	Jordanian	Arabic	Amman	Jordanian Dinar	Alia
Kenya	Kenyan	English Kiswahili	Nairobi	Kenya Shilling	Kenya Airways
Kuwait	Kuwaiti	Arabic	Kuwait	Kuwaiti Dinar	Kuwait Airways
Lebanon	Lebanese	Arabic French English	Beirut	Lebanese Pound	MEA (Middle East Airlines)
Libya	Libyan	Arabic	Tripoli	Dinar	Libyan Arab Airlines
Malaysia	Malaysian	Malay English	Kuala Lumpur	Malaysian Dollar	Malaysian Airline System
Malta	Maltese	Maltese English	Valletta	Maltese Pound	Air Malta
Mexico	Mexican	Spanish	Mexico City	Peso	Aeromexico Mexicana

Country	Adjective	Official Language(s)	Capital	Unit of Currency	Main International Airline(s)
Morocco	Moroccan	Arabic	Rabat	Dirham	Royal Air Maroc
The Netherlands	Dutch	Dutch	Amsterdam	Guilder	KLM (Royal Dutch Airlines)
New Zealand	New Zealand (person = a New Zealander)	English	Wellington	New Zealand Dollar	Air New Zealand
Nigeria	Nigerian	English	Lagos	Naira	Nigeria Airways
Norway	Norwegian	Norwegian	Oslo	Krone	SAS (Scandinavian Airlines)
Oman	Omani	Arabic	Muscat	Omani Riyal	Gulf Air
Pakistan	Pakastani	Urdu	Islamabad	Rupee	PIA (Pakistan International Airlines)
Peru	Peruvian	Spanish	Lima	Sol	Aero Peru
Philippines	Philippine (person = [a] Filipino)	Tagalog English	Manila	Peso	Philippine Airlines
Portugal	Portuguese	Portuguese	Lisbon	Escudo	TAP (Air Portugal
Qatar	Qatari	Arabic English	Doha	Qatar Riyal	Gulf Air
Saudi Arabia	Saudi (Arabian)	Arabic	Riyadh	Riyal	Saudia
Sierra Leone	Sierra Leonean	English	Freetown	Leone	Sierra Leone Airways
Singapore	Singaporean	English Chinese Malay Tamil	Singapore City	Singapore Dollar	Singapore Airlines
Scotland	Scottish (person = a Scot)	English	Edinburgh	Pound (Sterling)	British Airways British Caledonian
South Africa	South African	Afrikaans English	Pretoria	Rand	South African Airways
Spain	Spanish (person = a Spaniard)	Spanish	Madrid	Peseta	Iberia
Sri Lanka	Sri Lankan	Sinhalese Tamil English	Colombo	Rupee	Air Lanka
Sudan	Sudanese	Arabic English	Khartoum	Sudanese Pound	Sudan Airways
Sweden	Swedish (person = a Swede)	Swedish	Stockholm	Krona	SAS (Scandinavian Airlines)
Switzerland	Swiss	French German Italian	Berne	Swiss Franc	Swissair

Country	Adjective	Official Language(s)	Capital	Unit of Currency	Main International Airline(s)
Tanzania	Tanzanian	English Swahili	Dar Es Salaam	Tanzanian Shilling	Air Tanzania
Thailand	Thai	Thai Chinese English	Bangkok	Baht	Thai Airways
Tunisia	Tunisian	Arabic French	Tunis	Tunisian Dollar	Tunis Air
Turkey	Turkish (person = a Turk)	Turkish	Ankara	Turkish Lira	Turkish Airlines
Uganda	Ugandan	English Swahili	Kampala	Uganda Shilling	Uganda Airlines
United Arab Emirates	—	Arabic	Abu Dhabi	U.A.E. Dirham	Gulf Air
U.S.S.R. (Soviet Union)	Soviet	Russian	Moscow	Rouble	Aeroflot
U.K. (United Kingdom of Great Britain and Northern Ireland)	British	English	London	Pound (Sterling)	British Airways British Caledonian
U.S.A. (United States of America)	American	English	Washington	Dollar	American Airlines Delta North West Orient Pan Am (Pan American) TWA (Trans World Airlines)
Venezuela	Venezuelan	Spanish	Caracas	Bolivar	Venezuelan International Airways
Wales	Welsh	English Welsh	Cardiff	Pound (Sterling)	—
Yugoslavia	Yugoslavian (person = [a] Yugoslav)	Serbo-Croat	Belgrade	Dinar	Yugoslav Airlines
Zambia	Zambian	English	Lusaka	Kwacha	Zambia Airways
Zimbabwe	Zimbabwean	English Ndbele Shona	Harare	Zimbabwe Dollar	Air Zimbabwe

Metric Conversion

Length

U.K. & U.S.A.		metric
1 inch (in)		= 2.5 centimetres (cm)
1 foot (ft)	= 12 inches (in)	= 0.3 metres (m)
1 yard (yd)	= 3 feet (ft)	= 0.9 m
1760 yards (yd)	= 1 mile (mi)	= 1.6 kilometres (km)

metric		U.K. & U.S.A.
1 cm		= 0.4 in
1 m	= 100 cm	= 1.1 yd
1 km	= 1000 m	= 0.6 mi

Weight

U.K. & U.S.A.		metric
1 ounce (oz)		= 28.3 grams (gm)
1 pound (lb)	= 16 ounces (oz)	= 0.4 kilograms (km)
1 stone	= 14 lb	= 6.3 kg

metric		U.K. & U.S.A.
1 gm		= 0.04 oz
1 kg	= 1000 gm	= 2.2 lb

Liquid Measure

U.K.		metric
1 pint (pt)		= 0.6 litres (l)
1 gallon (gal)	= 8 pt	= 4.5 l

U.S.A.		metric
1 pt		= 0.47 liters (l)
1 gal	= 8 pt	= 3.8 l

metric	U.S.A.	U.K.
1 litre	= 2.1 pt	= 1.7 pt

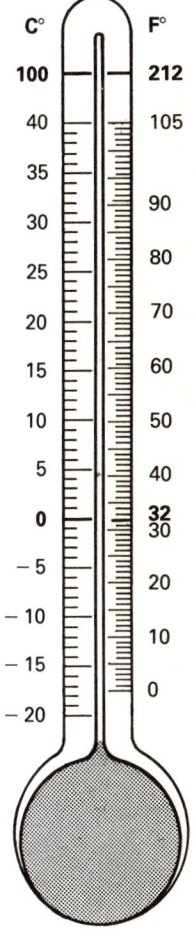

Temperature

To convert centigrade into degrees Fahrenheit, multiply centigrade by 1.8 and add 32.

To convert Fahrenheit into degrees centigrade, subtract 32 from Fahrenheit and divide by 1.8.

Alphabet Lists

2 useful standard codes for clarifying spellings over the telephone
e.g. "My name's Jane Beaton – that's B for Bravo, E for Echo, A for Alpha," etc.

A — Alpha		A — Andrew	
B — Bravo		B — Benjamin	
C — Charlie		C — Charlie	
D — Delta		D — David	
E — Echo		E — Edward	
F — Foxtrot		F — Frederick	
G — Glove		G — George	
H — Hotel		H — Harry	
I — India		I — Isaac	
J — Juliet		J — Jack	
K — Kilo		K — King	
L — Lima		L — Lucy	
M — Mike		M — Mary	
N — November		N — Nellie	
O — Oscar		O — Oliver	
P — Papa		P — Peter	
Q — Quebec		Q — Queenie	
R — Romeo		R — Robert	
S — Sierra		S — Sugar	
T — Tango		T — Tommy	
U — Uniform		U — Uncle	
V — Victor		V — Victor	
W — William		W — William	
X — X-ray		X — Xmas	
Y — Yankie		Y — Yellow	
Z — Zulu		Z — Zebra	